MURDER AT THE PRESIDENT'S HOUSE

By John R. Johnson

TEXT COPYRIGHT © 2014 John R. Johnson
All Rights Reserved

DEDICATION

To Jacque who inspire me to pursue my writing with a burning passion.

PROLOGUE

Murder at the President's House is a fictional account based loosely on the Murder in the White House by Margaret Truman and a thriller adaptation 1997 action film starring Wesley Snipes *Murder at 1600* directed by Dwight H. Little. The 1600 in the movie title refers to 1600 Pennsylvania, the address of the White House in Washington, DC. The film is based on Margaret Truman novel, daughter of U.S. President Harry S. Truman. From the outside, the President's House appears charmingly and deceptively modest. Except for unobtrusive office wings, it remains in structural outline just as it looked when it was basically completed in Jackson's day.

The **White House Counsel** is a staff appointee of the President of the United States whose principal role is to advise the President on all legal issues concerning the President and his Administration. The Office of Counsel to the President was created in 1943, and is responsible for advising on all legal aspects of policy questions, legal issues arising in connection with the President's decision to sign or veto legislation, ethical questions, financial disclosures and conflicts of interest during employment and post employment.

The Counsel's Office also helps define the line between official and political activities, oversees executive appointments and judicial selection, handles President pardons, reviews legislation and Presidential statements, and lawsuits against the President in his role as President, as well as serving the White House contact for the Department of Justice.

The White House Counsel offers legal advice to the President in his official capacity to the President, and does not serve as the President's personal attorney. In some instances, controversy has emerged over the scope of the attorney-client privilege between the Counsel and the President. Attorney-client privilege is an American legal concept that protects certain communications between a client and his or her attorney and keeps those communication confidential. The attorney-client privilege is one of the oldest recognized privileges for confidential communications. It is clear, however, that the privilege does not apply in personal matters such as impeachment proceedings thus, in such situations the President relies on a personal attorney for confidential legal advice.

There have been thirty seven (37) men appointed as the White House Counsel. The first was Samuel Irving Rosenman (1943-1946) serving under Presidents Franklin D. Roosevelt and Harry S. Truman. The current White House Counsel W. Neil Eggleston since June 1, 2014 under President Barack Obama.

TABLE OF CONTENTS

CHAPTER 1   A WEAPON OF CHOICE

CHAPTER 2   THE INVESTIGATION

CHAPTER 3   THE SEARCH IS ON

CHAPTER 4   EXODUS

CHAPTER 5   REQUIEM

CHAPTER ONE

A WEAPON OF CHOICE

> "And when you shall hear of rumors of wars, be not troubled; These things must needs to come to pass, the end is not yet." **Mark 13:7**

In the most powerful city in the world where the weapon of choice in a town such as this usually there are well aimed targeted rumors. Persistent rumors have abounded that First Lady Ashley Reid was having an affair with White House Counsel Richard Royster. No one can escape these rumors not even the leader of the free world.

Sometimes these rumors are true. Do you really want to know the truth?

An interesting rumor was leaked to the Washington Post occurred resulting in the front page headline, " **Ashley Reid Caught Having a Midnight Swim with White House Counsel**"

One of the distinguished members of the White House Press Corps had the nerve to ask the President the proverbial question. The President responded, "This is totally ridiculous and who leaked it is clearly a narcissistic loony toon." The First Lady is both a devoted mother and a cutthroat strategist. The President had , concluded his press conference on a hot summer Friday afternoon in June. He was preparing to leave the White House for the presidential retreat at Camp David.

Camp David is the country retreat of the President of the United States. It is located in the wooded hills about sixty-two (62) miles north-northwest of Washington, D.C., in Catoctin Mountain Park near Thurmont, Maryland. It is officially known as Naval Support Facility Thurmont and is technically a military installation; staffing is provided by the U.S. Navy and the U.S. Marine Corps. Construction was started in 1935 and completed in 1938. In 1942, it was converted to a presidential retreat by Franklin D. Roosevelt and renamed "**Shangri-La** "(for the fictional Himalayan paradise).

o

Camp David received its present name from Dwight D. Eisenhower, in honor of his father and grandson, both named David. Camp David is not open to the general public. Catoctin Mountain Park does not indicate the location of Camp David on its official park maps due to privacy and security concerns.

Thomas Jefferson Reid, President of the United States. He was forty-seven years old and looked maybe four years longer in his first term in office. He thrived on the presidency. Although his face was deeply lined, his hair was thick and dark. He was hard and thin to abrupt decisive movement.

Ashley Reid, First Lady was forty-six and looked thirty. She acknowledged a Hollywood surgeon had done creative restoration around her face and subdued some wrinkles, and the she said "she would have it done again whenever she thought she needed it."

President Reid turned away from the media group and herded his party towards the presidential helicopter, Marine One. He wavered and brightly grinned to the crowd. He and the First Lady, Charlotte, the First Daughter climbed into the waiting helicopter. The rotor was turning slowly above the helicopter. The red lights on it was blinking. **Marine One** is the call sign of any United States Marine Corps aircraft carrying the President of the United States. It usually denotes a helicopter operated by Marine Helicopter Squadron One (HMX-1 "Nighthawks"), either the large VH-3D Sea King or the newer, smaller VH-60N "Whitehawk". A Marine Corps aircraft carrying the Vice President has the call sign **Marine Two** .

The first use of helicopters for presidential transport in 1957, when President Dwight D. Eisenhower traveled on a Bell UH-13J Sioux.

The President needed a quick mode of transportation in order to reach his summer home in Gettysburg, Pennsylvania, as Air Force One could not land at either the White House or the summer home due to its sheer size. President Eisenhower instructed his staff to look into alternative modes of transportation and a Sikorsky UH-34 Seahorse helicopter was commissioned. The early aircraft lacked the "creature comforts" found on it modern successors, such as air conditioning and

o

toilets for in-flight use. In 1958, the H-13 was replaced by Sikorsky H-34, and in 1961 by the VH-3A. Not long after the mode of transportation was introduced, presidential aides the Marine Corps to look into the White House South Lawn as a helicopter landing zone. Ample room was present on the South Lawn, and the protocol was established.

Until 1976, the Marine Corps shared the responsibility of helicopter transportation for the President with the United States Army. Army helicopters used the call sign Army One while the president was on board. The VH-3D replaced some VH-3As in 1978, and the remaining VH-3As were replaced by the VH-60N beginning in 1987. Improvements were made to both types of helicopters since their introduction to take advantage of technological developments as well as to meet new mission critical requirements.

DIVERSITY is the real keynote to the 42 Presidents as a group. In physical appearance, temperament, place of birth, family background, role in national life, status of health, political affiliation, the nature and success of their administrations, popular reaction of their times and posterity toward them, and pursuits in later life, they demonstrate exceptional heterogeneity. Yet, in numerous respects, they exhibit similarities.

Chief among these is ethnic origin. All the President of the United States have been of Northern European extraction and preponderant number of British origins. English bloodlines predominate, followed by Scotch and Scotch-Irish. Both of Kennedy's parents were of Irish background. Although several Chief Executives carried traces of Continental European ancestry, the only one directly descended from that area were Van Buren and the two Roosevelts, whose names reflect their Dutch forebears; and Hoover and Eisenhower, both of Swiss-German lineage. Most of the parents of the Presidents and their families have spent generations in the United States; only a handful of Chief Executives, who by law are required to be American born, were the children of one or both immigrants parents.

A second area of resemblance is in occupation, where public service and the law ranks high. Except for Taylor, Grant and Eisenhower, who had been Army generals and whose earlier careers were essentially apolitical, practically all the Presidents played extensive roles in public life on the Federal, State, and local, appointive and elective. The range is considerable large, however Buchanan, for example, enjoyed almost four decades of experience in both State and Federal posts, including the diplomatic corps.

On the other hand, the only earlier elective office Arthur ever held was as Vice President. Lincoln's experience consisted only of four terms in the State legislature and a single term in the United States House of Representatives. Hoover, along with Taylor, Grant and Eisenhower never ran for any public office prior to his Presidential nomination, though he had served as Secretary of Commerce, as World War I Food Administrator, and on various national and international relief commissions.

Thirteen Chief Executives (John Adams, Jefferson, Van Buren, Tyler, Fillmore, Andrew Johnson, Arthur, Theodore Roosevelt, Coolidge, Truman, Lyndon B. Johnson, Nixon and Ford) had served as Vice Presidents. Nine were Cabinet members, Monroe holding two posts: six secretaries of State(Jefferson, Madison, Monroe, John Quincy Adams, Van Buren, and Buchanan); three Secretaries of War (Monroe, Grant and Taft); and one Secretary of Commerce(Hoover). Other Presidents also held various sub-Cabinets posts and lesser U.S. Government positions.

Seven served as Ambassadors or Ministers: both Adamses, Jefferson, Monroe, Van Buren, Harrison, and Buchanan--all before the Civil War. Taft held the position of Governor General of the Philippines; and after his Presidency, the Chief Justiceship of the United States, the only President who ever held a seat on the U.S. Supreme Court.

Except for twelve (12), the rest enjoyed congressional experiences, all before their incumbents except for John Quincy Adams who held a seat in the House of Representatives afterward, as did also Andrew Johnson in the Senate. The first five had served in the Continental Congress. The last two of these, Madison and Monroe, also sat in Congress, the former in the House and the latter in the Senate.

o

Ten (10) served in both Houses(John Quincy Adams, Jackson, William Henry Harrison, Tyler, Pierce, Buchanan, Andrew Johnson, Kennedy, Lyndon B. Johnson and Nixon); five in the Senate only(Monroe, Van Buren, Benjamin Harrison, Harding, and Truman); and eight in the House (Madison, Polk, Fillmore, Lincoln, Hayes, Garfield, McKinley, and Ford).

Polk was the only Speaker of the House to become Chief Executive. Tyler held the office of President pro tem of the Senate for one session. Lyndon B. Johnson served as both Minority and Majority Leader of the Senate. Garfield, and Ford were House Minority Leaders. Garfield was the only Chief Executive elected while serving as a Member of the House, though he was also a Senator-elect. Ford was appointed as Vice President while in the House, and then assumed the Presidency upon Nixon's resignation. Harding and Kennedy were elected while sitting in the Senate.

Sixteen (16) individuals had earlier served as Governors of States or Territories: Jefferson, Monroe, Jackson, William Henry Harrison, Van Buren, Tyler, Polk, Andrew Johnson, Hayes, Cleveland, McKinley, Theodore Roosevelt, Wilson, Coolidge, Franklin D. Roosevelt, and Carter. Four were Governors when they became President (Hayes, Cleveland, Wilson, and Franklin D. Roosevelt), and McKinley had left office earlier in the year that he ran for the Presidency.

Many White House occupants also served in State legislatures or held such State posts as attorney general, Lieutenant Governor, and comptroller, as well and county and city positions. Despite the prominence of large cities in U.S. history, only one mayor of a major city (Buffalo), Cleveland, ever occupied the highest office in the land.

More than two-thirds of the Presidents received training in the law, many in the days before formal school training when they "read the law.' Most of the overall group were admitted to the bar. Some curtailed or abandoned law practice during long periods in public office and never returned to actively. Wilson, for one stopped practicing after a short time, to begin graduate studies in political science.

o

Several men, including Van Buren, Hayes, Cleveland, Benjamin Harrison, McKinley, Taft, and Coolidge, worked as county or city prosecuting attorneys or solicitors before they entered the mainstream of political life. Jackson held the position of attorney general of the Western District of North Carolina (present day Tennessee) as well as justice of the Tennessee superior court. Taft also sat on a superior court, in Ohio, and was a Federal circuit judge.

A number of individuals were once elementary or secondary school teachers: John Adams, Jackson, Fillmore, Pierce, Garfield, Arthur, Cleveland (at a school for the deaf), McKinley, Harding, and Lyndon B. Johnson, Arthur and Johnson also served as principals. Of the group, Garfield moved on to college teaching, the one-time principal occupation of John Quincy Adams, Taft, and Wilson, Garfield, Wilson, and Eisenhower, respectively, served as presidents of Western Reserve Eclectic Institute (later Hiram College) and Princeton and Columbia Universities. Taft was dean of the Cincinnati Law School.

Several President were, by principal occupation, farm or plantation owners or managers, and those who engaged in other professions sometimes pursued agriculture as an avocation. Theodore Roosevelt, for example, though from an urban background, operated ranches in North Dakota. Other Chief Executives purchased or inherited family farms or estates.

Other occupations include mining engineer (Hoover), tailor (Andrew Johnson), and newspaper editor (Harding). A considerable number of Chief Executives were professional or semi professional soldiers. None were doctors or ministers, though William Henry Harrison studied medicine for a while; and John Adams and Madison theology.

During the course of their careers, numerous President followed humble occupations and knew disappointment and failure. Fillmore worked as a wool carder. Grant, as a young officer unhappy with military service, resigned and worked as a clerk and real estate agent, but he was unsuccessful in these fields as well as farming. Truman failed in haberdashery business, as did Lincoln in

o

storekeeping. A number of others at some point in their lives particularly during their early years, were forced to work at menial jobs.

Another general similarity among the Presidents is that, despite the modest origins of many of them, a great number were either wealthy or well-to-do as they neared the ends of their lives. Hoover and Lyndon B. Johnson were self-made millionaires. Franklin D. Roosevelt and Kennedy. by inheritance. Others Who enjoyed considerable wealth include Washington, Van Buren, Tyler , Polk, Taylor, Fillmore, Arthur, Benjamin Harrison, Theodore Roosevelt, Taft, Wilson, Harding, Coolidge, Truman, Eisenhower, and Nixon. On the other hand, Jefferson died in debt and Madison and Monroe ended their lives in genteel poverty, though all three always lived in comfortable circumstances. A few others also no more than modest wealth. At one point in his life, McKinley barely avoided bankruptcy.

Most Chief Executives have been well educated. The contrast are marked, however, Lincoln enjoyed only a few months of low-level formal education, whereas Wilson earned his Doctor of Philosophy (Ph.D.), the only Chief Executive to do so. Although historically speaking relatively few Americans have ever enjoyed the privilege of a college education, twenty-seven (27), or just over two-thirds, of the Presidents were graduates, and two others attended higher-level institutions but did not earn a degree. Of the 27, at least won honors or other academic distinction.

Five have been graduates of Harvard (the two Adams, two Roosevelts and Kennedy), two of the College of William and Mary (Jefferson and Tyler); two of Princeton (College of New Jersey) (Madison and Wilson); two of the U.S. Military Academy (Grant and Eisenhower); and 14 of other schools (Polk, University of North Carolina; Pierce, Bowdoin College; Buchanan, Dickinson College; Hayes, Kenyon College; Garfield, Williams College; Arthur, Union College; Benjamin Harrison, Miami (Ohio) University; Taft, Yale University; Harding, Ohio Central College; Coolidge, Amherst College; Hoover, Stanford University; Lyndon B. Johnson, Southwest Texas State Teachers College; Nixon, Whittier College; Ford, University of Michigan; and Carter, U.S. Naval Academy). A few of these

o

individuals also studied at other colleges or universities on a preparatory or temporary basis.

Those attending colleges but not graduating were Monroe (College of William and Mary), William Henry Harrison (Hampden-Sydney College), and William McKinley (Allegheny College). The following nine (9) men did not attend at all: Washington, Jackson, Van Buren, Taylor, Fillmore, Lincoln, Andrew Johnson, Cleveland, and Truman.

Wilson earned his Ph,D, in political science at John Hopkins. Except for John Adams, who received an M.A. from Harvard, no President ever was awarded one, though many of them won honorary degrees. Two undertook university-level study abroad briefly: John Quincy Adams at Holland's University of Leyden, and Kennedy at the London School of Economics. Madison accomplished a year of additional study at the College of New Jersey (now Princeton) following his graduation, as did also Franklin D. Roosevelt at Harvard.

Many Chief Executives undertook specialized professional training, particularly in the field of law. Graduates of law schools were Hayes (Harvard University), Taft (Cincinnati Law School), Wilson (University of Virginia), Nixon (Duke University), and Ford (Yale University). Those who attended schools but did not obtain degrees were McKinley (Albany Law School), both Roosevelts (Columbia University), Truman (Kansas City Law School), and Lyndon B. Johnson (Georgetown University).

The following read law in the days before formal legal training was available or commonplace: both Adamses, Jefferson, Madison, Monroe, Jackson, Van Buren, Tyler, Polk, Fillmore, Pierce, Buchanan, Lincoln, Garfield, Arthur, Cleveland, Benjamin Harrison, Harding, and Coolidge. In addition, at least three of those who matriculated at law schools---Hayes, McKinley, and Taft--also read law.

Another marked similarity is in the performance of military service. Twenty-four (24), or about two-thirds of the Presidents have served in various branches of the Armed Forces or state militia units, one, Buchanan, in a private volunteer group during the War of 1812. Interestingly enough, all except him attained officer status, eleven (11) as generals. A few worked their way up from enlisted ranks. Three became commanders of the Army: Washington, Grant, and Eisenhower.

For at least 11, notable success as officers provided a stepping stone on their way to the Presidency: Washington, Jackson, William Henry Harrison, Taylor, Pierce, Grant, Hayes, Garfield, Benjamin Harrison, Theodore Roosevelt, and Eisenhower-- only three of whom (Taylor, Grant and Eisenhower) were professional soldiers for the major part of their lives. The only erstwhile naval personnel among the Chief Executives have been the last five Presidents (Kennedy, Lyndon B. Johnson, Nixon, Ford and Carter), all of whom served as officers below the admiral rank.

Despite the trend toward urbanization in the United States from its earliest days, the Presidents have overwhelmingly hailed from small towns and rural areas. , Only Theodore Roosevelt, Taft, Kennedy, and Ford were born in metropolitan areas or large cities. A number who came from rural areas, including Jackson, Polk, Fillmore, Buchanan, Lincoln, and Garfield, as well as possibly Taylor and Pierce, literally rose from "log cabins " to the White House. Most of the others were born in modest homes amid humble or middle-class surroundings. Van Buren was born in his father's tavern. A few individuals of agrarian origins belonged to well-to-do families; or they and members of their families subsequently advanced to positions of wealth and prominence.

In line with the predominance of rural origins, the fathers of more than the Presidents were, at one time or another, farmers or plantations owners. Others were professional men or executives, including several lawyers, clergymen, teachers, and financiers. Additional diverse occupations include: ironmaker, livestock dealer, carpenter, blacksmith, tanner, tavern keeper, surveyor, mechanic, storekeeper, merchant, and tavern porter.

According to a recent survey of nearly 70 people who lived a century or longer revealed that the best United States President of the past 100 years to nearly 40 percent of the group was Franklin D. Roosevelt.

When a New President of the United States take office and moves into the White House, he enters a dwelling that is a home, office, and goldfish bowl as well a "protective bubble" all in one. The president's family must get used to it, he must do the best he possibly can within it and in spite of it. He is never far from crowds or the glare of the limelight, and at times he must surely be the loneliest man in America, when he is called on to sit alone and make a decision that may change the course of both American and world history.

The President is the people possession for four years or eight years in some cases: when he speaks. he speaks for the people, and the White House has long echoes in its hallways and corridors. For example, the White House gets part of its tone from one President who never lived in it--George Washington.

For an executive mansion he had an imposing town house in New York and then in Philadelphia. He held "levees" after the royal manner, with powdered footmen in the entrance hall. He lived in a style intended to prove that the Chief Executive of the United States was a person of great importance.

In recent decades the world has drawn much closer to the White House. Perhaps it would not be too much to say that the heads of states of foreign nations take an alert in what happens there as the governor of the several states did in the old days. Still the White House is a peculiarly American institution. It reflects the personality of the man who occupies the White House, it also reflects the total personality of the people who voted and put him there. It is their own special possession and symbol, embodying what they have hoped for and dreamed of and want to live up to.

Still the man who lives in the White House must find the care of the of office as inescapable as his own flesh and bone. To talk to a friend who has a new baby to welcome or death to mourn, he may to snatch moments from planning an international conference.

The White House which is the central Executive Residence, flanked by the East Wing West Wing as well as Office Building-the former State Department which now houses offices for the President's staff and the Vice President--and Blair House, a guest residence. The Chief Usher coordinates the day to day household functional operations at the White House.

The White House includes a building comprising six stories and 55,000 square feet, 132 rooms and 35 bathrooms, 412 doors, 147 windows, twenty-eight fireplaces, eight staircases, three elevators, five full-time chefs, a tennis court, a single lane bowling alley(officially called the Harry S. Truman Bowling Alley), a movie theater(officially the White House Family Theater), a jogging track, a swimming pool, a putting green. It receives up to 30,000 visitors each a week. - the Ground Floor, State Floor, Second Floor, and Third Floor, as well as a two-story basement. The White House was constructed on October 13, 1792, the house was designed by James Hoban of white painted Aquia Creek sandstone in the Neoclassical Palladian style.

On Saturday, November 1, 1800, John Adams became the first president to take up residence in the building. During Adam's second day in the White House, he wrote a letter to his wife Abigail, containing a prayer for the house. President Adams wrote:

" I pray Heaven to bestow the best of blessings on this House, and all that shall hereafter inhabit it. May none but honest and wise men ever rule under this roof."

o

Franklin D. Roosevelt had Adams's blessing carved into the mantel in the State Dining Room.

When Thomas Jefferson moved into the house into the house in 1801, he (with architect Benjamin Henry Latrobe) expanded the building outward creating two colonnades that were meant to conceal stables and storage areas.

In 1814, during the War of 1812, the executive mansion was set ablaze by the British Army in the Burning of Washington, destroying the interior and charring much of the exterior. Reconstruction began almost immediately, and President James Monroe moved into the partially reconstructed Executive Residence in October 1817. Construction continued with the addition of the South Portico in 1824 and the North in 1829. Because of crowding within the executive mansion itself, President Theodore Roosevelt had all work offices relocated to the newly constructed West Wing in 1901. Eight years later, President Williams Howard Taft expanded the West Wing and created the first Oval Office which was eventually moved as the section was expanded. The third floor attic was converted to living quarters in 1927 by augmenting the existing hip roof with long shed dormers. A newly constructed East Wing was used as a reception area for social events; Jefferson's colonnades connected the new wings. East Wing alterations were completed additional office space. By 1948, the house's load bearing exterior walls and internal wood beams exterior walls and internal wood beams were found to be close to failure. Under President Harry S. Truman, the interior rooms were completely dismantled and a new internal load bearing steel frame constructed inside the walls. Once this work was completed, interior rooms were rebuilt.

The term *White House* is often used a metonym for the Executive Office of the President of the United States and for the president's administration and advisers in general, as in "The White House had decided that…"

The property is a National Heritage Site owned by the National Park Service and is part of the President's Park.

o

The White House Complex is protected by the United States Secret Service and the United States Park Police.

NASAMS (Norwegian Advanced Surface to Air Missile System) were used to guard airspace over Washington, D.C. during the 1992 presidential inauguration. The same NASAMS units have since been used to protect the president and all air space around the White House which is strictly prohibited to aircraft. For security reasons, the section of Pennsylvania Avenue in front of the White House is closed to all vehicular traffic, except government officials.

Marine One is sometimes the preferred alternative to presidential motorcades, which can be expensive and logistically difficult. The controlled environment of a helicopter adds greatly to the safety factor as well. It is used to transport senior Cabinet staff and foreign dignitaries.

The rotor rung fast and the helicopter rose several hundreds of feet off the ground.. The copter hovered above the ground. Two others just like it rose and joined it, before it gained attitude and left the area of the White House complex.

The other two helicopters gunships carrying heavy duty electronics to detect any threat to the presidential helicopter from a missile, from an airplane, from a shot fired from the ground, and to take electronic countermeasures to the fired shot if necessary.

The Presidential helicopter flew on the left side of the formation this particular afternoon. Sometimes it flew in the middle, sometimes on the right. An attacker would not know which helicopter carried the President on board of it. This has been referred to as a presidential shell game. As a security measure Marine One always flies in a group with identical helicopters as many as five.

Marine aviators flying Marine One do not wear flight suits during flights, but rather the Marine Blue Dress Charlie/Delta uniform. More than 800 Marine supervise the operation of the Marine One fleet, which is based in MCAF Quantico, Virginia,

o

with additional operating location at Naval Support Facility Anacostia in the District of Columbia, but is more often seen in action on the South Lawn of the White House. At Joint Base Andrews Naval Facility in Maryland, it is sometimes used to connect to Air Force for longer journeys. Marine One is met on the ground by at least one Marine in full dress uniform(most often two with one acting as an armed guard).

Marine One is also equipped with standard military anti-missile countermeasures such as flares to counter heat-seeking missiles and chaff to counter radar-guided missiles, as well as AN/ALQ-14A infrared countermeasures. HMX-1 operates a total of thirty-five (35) helicopters of four differents types.

To add to the security of Marine One, every member of HMX-1 is required to pass a Yankee White background check before touching any of the helicopters used for presidential travel.

Marine One is transported via C-17 or C-5 military transport planes(as is the president's limousine) wherever the President travels, within the U.S. as well as overseas. At presidential inauguration, the Marines offer the outgoing President a final flight from the U.S. Capitol to Joint Base Andrews Naval Air Facility. Marine One has not been the subject of any accident or attack through 1993.

On June 20, 1993 five months to the day Thomas Jefferson Reid took office as President of the United States, the White House Counsel Richard Royster day began with nothing out of the ordinary. He decide to forgo his morning jog, and his wife Rebecca described his demeanor that day as better than it had been" in a while." Royster left for work promptly at about 8:00 a.m. Rebecca saw him for the last time standing "stiffly" in the kitchen.

She kissed him goodbye in their quaint kitchen, as he left their Georgetown home driving his 1990 silver-gray Honda Accord which bore Tennessee license plates. On the way to the White House, he dropped his daughter, Jessica, off at work and his son, Robert, at the Dupont Circle metro station for the Scholastic Aptitude Test preparation course.

o

He arrived a bit later than usual to his office, at 8:50 a.m. rather than his customarily punctual 8:00 a.m. He had time to grab a cup of coffee and a bran muffin before attending the 9:00 a.m. morning meeting of the White House Counsel office staff. After the meeting ended, he attended a White House ceremony announcing the appointment of William Freeman to replace Dennis Reed, who had been fired amidst allegations of ethical improprieties the day before. It was the first time in history a president had fired a head of the FBI, Reed would later declare his firing had "seriously compromised" the Royster investigation.

Before Linda Jones left the office for her lunch hour, she asked if there was anything she could do for her boss "No," Royster said, "I believe I have everything,. I need"
Jones said, "Yes sir, I will see you later after lunch." Royster responds, "Have a nice lunch Linda."

After reading the The Washington Post, newspaper for a few minutes, he then decides to go out to lunch at his favorite restaurant in Georgetown, The Daily Grill. He told his secretary Jones"I will be back after lunch."

He walked out of his office after offering his co-worker Deborah Smith some leftover M&M's from his official White House candy jar. He was wearing his Brooks Brothers navy blue pinstripe suit, white shirt with striped tie and black Johnston Murphy wing tips shoes upon his departure from his office. Royster did not carry his leather monogrammed briefcase or anything else in his hands to lunch.

As Royster left the White House he passed by Secret Service agent Robert Gates, the last person known to have seen the White House Counsel alive.
"How are you doing, sir?" Gates asked.
"Fine," Royster replied, giving the agent a half smile as he walked off, out of the door of the White House.

o

Upon his arrival at the Daily Grill at 1310 Wisconsin Avenue NW, in which the Georgetown Inn is conveniently located with the premises. Royster turned off his cell phone to avoid any interruptions while having his lunch on that particular day away his office. A number of people tried unsuccessfully to reach him by cell phone. One missed call showed up on his cell phone, C. Grantham Hunt, Royster's former partner at the Hart Law Firm called to discuss finalizing work that Hunt had been doing to set up a blind trust for the Reid's. Royster, who was acting as Hunt's contact point at the White House, was supposed to have the Reid's sign some documents to complete the process.
Hunt stated that there was nothing about the blind trust that would have provided a source of concern to Royster, nor did Royster ever express any concern.

He dined heartedly on a California chicken burger, French fries, kale caesar salad complimented with a Sea Breeze. He finished his lunch and hailed down a cab at the corner of M Street & Wisconsin Avenue NW, returning to his office at the White House at 2:00 p.m.

Contrary to the White House spin, Richard Royster's connection to the Reid's was primarily via Ashley rather than Tom, Richard and Ashley had been partners at the Hart law firm and allegations of an outgoing affair had persisted from Memphis days to the White House itself.

Richard Royster had been struggling with the Presidential Blind Trust that normally is a trivial matter, the trust had been delayed for five months and the U.S. Trustee was beginning to make noises. One of the requirements imposed on the Presidency is that the personal wealth of the First Family be placed in a blind trust for the term of office. The reasons for this step should be obvious. The First Family, with access to inside information, is in a position to personally profit quite handsomely from that information. There is a name for that. It is called "insider trading" and it's a crime.

The reason that the trust is "blind" with the First Family unaware of just exactly how their funds are invested, is to prevent awareness of personal wealth from influencing matters of National Policy.

o

Since its inception, each President has had the blind trust completed and in the hands of a trustee at the time of the President's inauguration as required.

With one exception.

The trust declarations for Thomas Reid's assets were not delivered to the trustee's office on Inauguration Day. Or the day after that, or the next week, or the week after that, or the next month, or the month after that!

On June 20, 1993, five months to the day after Tom Reid vowed to preserve, protect, and defend the United States Constitution, the trust declarations still languished, unfinished, on the desk of the man tasked to complete them, the White House Counsel Richard Royster.

It is a minor but salient point that that the blind trust is considered the President's personal business, to be completed with his own lawyer prior to assuming the Office of the Presidency. As Richard Royster was part of the White House staff, and paid for by the taxpayer, it was inappropriate for him to be working on Reid's personal business. Admittedly a technical matter, but germaine in all essence of the word.

But, appropriate or not, Royster had the job of completing the six month late blind trust declarations.

What is a trust declaration? A trust declaration is a list. A list of assets. A house. A condo. These bank accounts. Those stocks. The Reid's do not claim to be exceptionally wealthy compared to the other presidents. Indeed, the Reid's public posture is of relative poverty. Why then would a simple listing of their assets drag on for six months?

Richard Royster, the man tasked with making up that list of assets and submitting them, a delayed completion for 5 months. Why?

o

There is only one way that a list of assets can have a problem, and that if the list is incomplete, or fraudulent. As the preparer, had Richard Royster submitted trust declarations he knew to be incomplete or fraudulent, he would face criminal prosecution had the fraud were uncovered.

That the trust does not include all the Reid's assets regarding a file cabinet in the private residence with (among other items) paperwork on the Reid's "condominium", an asset should be under care of the trustees.

That assets would not be in the trust, and why?

Assets whose origins don't bear close scrutiny, for one. With recent revelations of highly questionable donations from Zippo Group, money laundering through a California Hindu Temple, and four dead 1992 Reid Campaign fundraisers, the reports of cash flowing from the CIA's gun and drug operations at Menu airport gain credibility. It certain that such tainted assets would not look on the trust declarations. That Reid took cash from at least two drug criminals is now proven fact.

The Reid's in particular Ashley, had a prior history of highly questionable stock and commodities trading practices, of which Pharmgate" is the most famous. A lesser known fact is that during the abortive health care reform, Ashley Reid made a small profit by short selling pharmaceutical stocks. That's insider trading, it's illegal, and it's the very activity the blind trust(still incomplete at the time) was intended to present.

Knowing the blind trust is fraudulent, and knowing that Royster was in a position to know of the fraud, his obvious reluctance to complete the declarations become quite understandable. Were the fraud ever revealed, Royster himself would face jail time. Submitting his resignation would be the preferable action.

That Royster's resignation would have been a problem is quite clear. It would have brought attention to the already late Presidential Blind Trust and what it contained, or to be more accurate, what it didn't contain.

o

Had Royster resigned, and the trust declarations been submitted anyway on the paperwork he had worked on, the same self-preservation that led him to resign would have forced him to speak out.

Had that happened, and investigation into the blind trust resulted, the money trail through the Reid's to NDFA, and back to Meni, would have been laid bare.

Royster was the sole keeper of the files regarding all Reid's Tennessee dealings.

Barry Johansen, and Johansen partner Darnell Miller a close friend of the Reid's had helped the Reid campaign by providing charter air service. After the election was over, Barry was everywhere in and around the White House, working on improving the First Couple's image. His disastrous meddling came when his partner Darnell told Barry he did hear the rumors that the White House Office of Communications was corrupt, and worse, disloyal to the First Family,(This happened in the time frame of the leaks about marital discord in the White House and everyone was ultra sensitive.) So Barry began pressing Ashley, telling her that the communications office people were "a bunch of crooks" and that ""we got to get to our own people in there."

Ashley Reid, in turn, pressed Richard Royster and Andre Watkins (who in her opinion of the matter were already failing her because of the leaks, the press, the secret service, etc.). Quickly, the whole messy ‚silly and crazy' Commgate' was in full swing.

Royster was also facing a possible a Congressional inquiry into his involvement into the firing of ten people from the White House Office of Communications, what would become as Commgate. It was one of the series of problems and scandals Royster was confronting not only in his role as White House Counsel but in his role as a personal lawyer for the Reid's. It all took a huge toll on Royster, and his wife and friends who sensed his gathering despair. In the end the terminated staffers

o

had pals in the press who wrote their story and suddenly Congress is talking about an investigation into the firing.

Royster had taken direct orders from Ashley Reid in the affair and faced charges that he was complicit with the Reid's in using FBI investigation to shake up the office and install friends in those positions.

Suddenly, the White House (it now April-May-June 1993) is on the defensive, trying to explain itself. At a press conference, George Stevens said the FBI had evidence the communications office were full of crooks and criminals-an assertion that the FBI disputes.

And then came the inevitable self-inquiry, led by White House Jay Poole which was aimed at pointing the finger some place besides at Ashley and her meddling friend Barry Johansen. In the end, Richard Royster got the blame and become the "Fall Guy" for the Reid administration.

Royster's role as presidential legal advisor, counsel, liaison and buffer zone can poses a bit too much for one man to handle at any given time in his life.

Life in the White House depressed Royster even further. One of Royster's jobs in the White House Counsel's Office was to vet new appointees. On the night that Reid's first nominees Warren Burd, was forced to withdraw for hiring illegal nannies. Royster was so full of self-reproach that he became physically sick. He began losing weight and he had difficulty sleeping.

All of this made Roster quite sick. He was integrally involved in Commgate, having been consulted by Andre Watkins because he was a lawyer too. He overseen the investigation of the ten White House Office of Communications employees(though he'd always been cautious about acting precipitously). He did participated meetings with the FBI. And most importantly, he'd discussed the problem with Ashley--who had impatiently asked "what's being done" about those crooked disloyal communications office people.

o

Over the course of several weeks, Royster, in his careful lawyerly, increasingly distressed fashion, laid out his case in a private chronology he kept in a spiral notebook. He did write down from his memory of events, consult his calendar, add things here and there. And then, he did write it all down again, over and over, narrowing, broadening,editing--obsessing, in other words. He plainly feared embarrassment and public humiliation in a Congressional hearing that he firmly believed coming. Through it all, he was clearly motivated by his pointed intention to protect Ashley Reid (AR)--The Client.

This is the first of two private review meetings written by Richard Royster, he had with Ashley Reid (AR) in which was plainly annoyed and eager for something to be done about the White House Office of Communications mess, she'd hearing about from Barry. Note that in recollecting her mood, Dick wrote to himself "general impatience", and then thought himself ungallant and changed "impatience" to "frustration."

: Q-Question
DK: Don't Know
WB-William Bell
AR-Ashley Reid

1st discussion-attempt to reconstruct
 go to see re AR, enterprise liab, visibility
Q- when will (AR) analysis be finished
DK-whether brought up mgmnt or wrongdoing
or both
[or she brought up/]   [or she brought up argument]
[and I brought up 2 segments wrongdoing] [and I brought up wrongdoing or just wrongdoing]
What's going on? Are you on top of it?
Trying to determine if there is actual wrongdoing

Assigned to WB
get frustration--I respond we just heard about it yesterday
(probably made me made at criticism and frustrated no auditors
Q did BJ say anything?

The is Dick's second retelling to himself, obviously in anticipation of some inquiry of his two meetings with Ashley. By this time, he edited out her mood, and has her asking a milder series of questions. ("Do you know anything about any problems with the Communications Office?" as

o

opposed to "Are you on top of it?")

: WB=William Bell
SS=Secret Service

2 conversation w/AR on Thurs

1st after late lunch
go to see her re med malpractice issue
 -could be on visibility of enterprise liability
(was conducting analysis of proposed reform
Q: how comm office come up?
Eg. do you know anything re any problems w comm office or , I've heard something about it " " " "

Told her had some (soft?) info assigned to WB

Q--anyone else present?
don't recall
sometimes persons present, sometimes not

Here, Dick sets out an imperative for himself; to defend the firing of the communications office workers, thereby defending whatever role Ashley might have had in it. It was clear he didn't think she could be completely from the firing, so the strategy became "defend the firing."

: AR=Ashley Reid
-Coordination

defend mgmnt decision
thereby defend AR role whatever it was in fact or might have been
misperceived to be

This is Dick's version of his meeting with Jay Poole about the in-house inquiry into Commgate, by which time the thing had blown up in everybody's faces and finger pointing time had come.

o

Privileged
 anticipation of litigation

:AR=Ashley Reid
DM=Darnell Miller
BJ=Barry Johansen
RR=Richard Royster

5/30/93

Poole mtg in my office

Johansen says he never talked to OR before Friday evening, had received prior info about her interest from me

DM is vague in memory when he talked to her but BJ believes she first mentioned it to DM shortly before the mtg w DM, BJ & RR on Thurs afternoon

I told Jay that after a late lunch on Thursday I spoke w/AR was primarily working on medical malpractice project at the time and could have been in discussion re same. She was aware of some assertions of impropriety in the communications office and wanted to know what was being done about it--I related I had given to Bell as our security officer.

Richard Royster's position as White House Counsel did not sit well with him, a true perfectionist who have never faced a career setback in his professional life. He graduated at the top of his class at the University of Tennessee Law School, scored highest in the state bar exam, and seemed to be at the pinnacle of his career before coming to Washington.

 Three weeks before his death, he told his brother-in-law Berry Hughes, Jr., a prominent Washington lawyer, " I spent a lifetime building reputation, and now I am in the process of having it tarnished." Closer to that fateful Friday, Royster asked his wife Rebecca, "How did I get myself into a mess like this?"

 Only days before following a public speech stressing the value of integrity. He confided with friends and family that he was thinking about resigning his position. Royster had even drafted an outline for his letter of resignation. Things had seemly gotten better for Royster lately, his wife wife recalled. They have spent a fun filled

o

weekend in Ocean City, MD beach shoreline and Royster had promised to take Rebecca on a date Friday evening.

Royster had scheduled a private meeting with Tom Reid for the very next day, June 22, 1993 at which it appeared, he intended to resign. He spent his last days paying bills and dutifully wrapping up the details of his father's estate.

Richard Royster had a spent the entire morning making "busy work" in his office and attended the White House announcement of William Freeman as the new head of the FBI earlier in the day(passing by the checkpoint manned by White House uniformed guard Bryce).

This is a key point. U.S. Secret Service tasked by Congress after the assassination of President William McKinley to protect the U.S. President, Vice President and their families since 1901 The agency virtually melted down into which appeared to be pool of incompetence or worse. As President, Tom Reid deals with many major issues that affect all of us--crime, drugs, and the environment, just to name a few here. However, when our 16th President, Abraham Lincoln (1861-1865), was in office, times was vastly different than now. President Lincoln is well known for his leadership during the Civil War and for signing the Emancipation Proclamation, which freed the slaves. However, did you know that he also established the United States Secret Service.

When the United States Secret Service (USSS) was established, its main duty was to prevent the illegal production, or counterfeiting, of money. In the 1800s, America's monetary system was very disorganized. Bills and coins were issued by each state through individual banks, which generated many types of legal currency. With so many different kinds of bills in circulation, it was very easy for people to counterfeit money. During President Lincoln's Administration, more than a third of the nation's money was counterfeit. On the advice of Secretary of the Treasury Hugh McCulloch, President Lincoln established a commission to stop this rapidly growing problem that was destroying the nation's economy, and on April 14, 1865, he created the United States Secret Service to carry out the commission's recommendations.

o

The Secret Service officially went to work on July 5, 1865. It first chief was William Wood. Chief Wood, widely known for his heroism during the Civil War, was very successful in his first year closing more than 200 counterfeiting plants. This success helped prove the value of the Secret Service, and in 1866 the National Headquarters was established in the Department of Treasury. During the evening of the same day President Lincoln established the Secret Service, he was assassinated at Ford's Theatre in Washington, D.C., by John Wilkes Booth. The country mourned as news spread that the President had been shot. It was the first time in our nation's history that a President had been assassinated. As cries from citizens rang out, Congress began to think about adding Presidential protection to the list of duties performed by the Secret Service. However, it would take 36 years and the assassination of two more Presidents---James A. Garfield (March 4,1881-September 10, 1881) and William McKinley (1897-1901)--before the Congress added protection of the President to the list of duties performed by the Secret Service.

Since 1901, every President from Theodore Roosevelt on has been protected by the Secret Service. In 1917, threats against the President became a felony (a serious crime in the eyes of the law), and Secret Service protection was broadened to include all members of the First Family. In 1951, protection of the Vice President and the President-elect was added. After the assassination of Presidential candidate Robert Kennedy in 1968, President Lyndon B. Johnson (1963-1969) authorized the Secret Service to protect all Presidential candidates.

Today's Secret Service is made up of two primary divisions--the Uniformed Division and the Special Agent Division. The primary role of the Uniformed Division is protection of the White House and immediate surroundings as well as the residence of the Vice President. Originally named the White House Police, the Uniformed Division was established by an Act of Congress on July 1, 1922, during President Warren G. Harding's Administration (1921-1923).
The Special Agent Division is charged with two missions: protection and investigation. During course of their careers, special agents carry out assignments

in both of these areas. Their many investigative responsibilities include counterfeiting, forgery, and financial crimes. In addition to protecting the President, the Vice President, and their immediate families, agents also provide protection for foreign heads of state and heads of government visiting the United States,

The White House is the most secure private residence in the world equipped with sophisticated entry control system and video surveillance installed by Mitre Corporation. There are twenty-seven (27) security cameras installed within the various surveillance points in the White House. The video surveillance records all comings and goings from the White House.

According to Roland Hynes, who retired after 30 years as a Maryland State Trooper, and who also served for ten years after an appointment to the state's governor to Homeland Security Review Committee.

"Anything is possible" Mr Hynes told the Washington Post I have worked with the Secret Service based on what I have seen there but I would doubt it, If you were to ask me what I do think is most likely the issue is incompetence or security protocol meltdown. Finally, I would honestly say incompetence is the major culprit.

He is referring to the Secret Service's special uniformed unit charged with protecting the White House, embassies, consulates, and chanceries. Although it had been the subject of considerable criticism because of its use of extensive manpower and excessive money to patrol Washington's safest streets and best neighborhoods-- while the Metropolitan Police Department had to deal with the city's worst crime infested areas--it had been considered a political sacred cow ever since Richard Nixon established it in 1969.

There has been a rash of troubling security failures by the Secret Service in the two weeks leading up to President Reid's White House meeting with Chinese Prime Minister Vincent Dinh.

o

Another hostile power possibly foreign has infiltrated and compromised the integrity of the U.S Secret Service Uniformed Division. The lone assassin posing as a member of the Secret Service to gain full access to the White House enter the premises undetected by physical security and stealth mode to the electronic security systems.

The killer proceeds swiftly to the office of the White House Counsel, briskly running up the steps to the second floor of the West Wing where the office of White House Counsel Richard Royster was located. He slips on a pair of latex examination gloves before opening Royster's office door. He rushes in the door, squeezing the trigger of his gun, firing the fatal shot striking Richard Royster in his head, killing him dead. The gunshots was unheard by staff working at the time within the building, due to the use of a silencer on the gunman's. 38 caliber revolver.

Several hours after he was last seen now Richard Royster, White House Counsel is dead. The first witness to arrive on the newly minted crime scene in Royster's office is Anna Chavez, a White House housekeeper.

.

Chavez discovers the dead body of Richard Royster slumped over at his desk in a pool of fresh blood of his office located on the second floor of the West Wing of the White House at 6:00 .pm. She screams at the top of her lungs at the sight of Royster's dead body. Chavez makes a mad dash out of the office to the nearest telephone in an empty office down the hallway, to make her distressing call, She immediately calls her supervisor who in turn called Richard Spriggs, Secret Service agent. Agent Spriggs ordered all White House entrances and exits be sealed off and locked down until further notice. Several Secret Service agents rushed to secure various White House sectors that is on security cameras throughout the building. It is just after 6:30 p.m. when the call comes into the 911 operator of the D.C. Metropolitan Police Department by Spriggs.

911 Operator: "How may I help you?
Spriggs: " I am Secret Service agent Spriggs calling to report a murder at the White House"
911 Operator: The White House 1600 Pennsylvania Ave is that correct address?
Spriggs: Affirmative

o

911 Operator I will send our officers and homicide detectives over promptly.
Spriggs: Thank you.

The 911 operator cautions him to not touch anything, and to close the office door and wait outside for the police to arrive on the scene. A note is handled off to the dispatcher, who then sends two patrol cars and an ambulance to the scene. While they are en route, the dispatcher calls the detective's office and advises the Duty Sergeant of the call.

She notices that there is a forensic unit already on the intersection of 4200 Connecticut Avenue NW, which had just cleared photographing an accident scene. The forensic people was taking a coffee break. She raises them on the radio and advises them of the homicide call, so they can come back to the station to pick up any equipment they may need at the scene.

The first D.C. Metropolitan Police patrol car arrives at the White House at 7:06 p.m. with the ambulance right behind it on its tail end. The two patrol officers have escorted the housekeeper to sit in their car while they enter the crime scene in the White House West Wing, guns drawn, to ensure that the killer is not still present in the residences, and to confirm whether the victim is still alive or not.

The second patrol car reaches the scene, to find one of the first officers on the scene interviewing the housekeeper, while inside of the White House building the other officer who has taken the job of controlling access to the scene speaks to the paramedics.

This officer has already led one of the paramedics into the scene, to assure him that the victim is beyond medical help. There are obvious gunshots wounds, including one to the head, so there is little question of the victim's status.

The paramedics are there to render medical assistance, and there is little hope for the victim. The police have the same attitude, but if the victim is beyond hope then they are expected to protect the crime scene from contamination. The officer

o

controlling access keeps detailed careful records of exactly who was in the scene and when.

He shows the notes to each person who enters and leaves, and asks them to sign to confirm its accuracy. He knows that few people should be allowed onto the crime scene, and should all use the same route while walking to avoid destroying any evidence unnecessarily. While this is going on the dispatcher has called the Chief Medical Examiner Jim A. Bayes to attend the scene.

Nothing can done with the body or the scene until the Medical Examiner or assistants has viewed it and declared the person to be deceased. In this case the Chief Medical Examiner Bayes checks Richard Royster for a pulse, checks the scene, and speaks briefly to the paramedics. He then tell the officer guarding the scene that he is pronouncing Royster to be deceased at 8:48 p.m., which the officer makes a note. He also advises the officer he is officially turning the death investigation over to the police as a homicide.

Meanwhile, the Duty Sergeant from the Detective's office has found that all of the General Assignment detectives he has are either busy in the city. or are already involved in important interviews which really shouldn't be interrupted. It has been a busy week, and he has no choice but to call in a detective from the day shift who was just about to go to bed. He tells him to come into the station and grab a car, and that he'll meet him at the scene.

The Duty Sergeant feels that he should personally visit the scene as soon as possible., since the presence of a detective with experience in major high profile crimes may prevent mistakes from being made by inexperienced patrol officers. He checks his computer screen before he leaves, to see who is at the scene. Nothing that one of the patrol contains two older experienced officers, his mind was put at ease.

The detective he has called in has major crime experience,so the Duty Sergeant's involvement will be minimal, and the next day another detective will be assigned to work with the Primary Investigator. He quickly calls the Staff Sergeant in charge of the Detective's Office at home to advise him of the situation at the White House.

The Duty Sergeant arrives at the crime scene to find the Chief Medical Examiner Jim Bayes and the paramedics just leaving. The Forensic Identification crew is standing by for permission to start photographing the scene. They have been to the station to picked cases of evidence collection equipment and supplies. Some things are already stored in their van, but some items(like for example extra film, and blood preservative test tubes) are temperature sensitive and can't be stored in a vehicle on a hot summer day.

He chats with the Chief Medical Examiner Bayes for a minute(they have met at crime scenes many times over a course of years), and then goes to speak to the officer guarding Richard Royster's office door. Taking a quick look at the body and the office, he then clears the Forensic officer to start photographing, but not to collect any evidence or disturb anything until the Primary Investigator for the case arrives on the scene.

He then goes outside and tells the second patrol crew that they won't be needed any more, and they can go back to patrol, but not until they've gone on a coffee run at Dunkin Donuts. It's going to be a long night, and rest of the people involved won't be going home at midnight like they had expected.

The Forensic team had followed him out, and has put on disposable "bunny suits", biohazard coveralls to prevent them from inadvertently coming in contact with blood or bodily fluids. Once they start collecting evidence, they put on latex gloves.

The Duty Sergeant then talks to the officer who was interviewing the housekeeper. He had a taken a detailed statement from her. The Staff Sergeant reads the officer's notes, and then briefly speaks to the woman, ascertaining that she has someone (her husband) at home. He advises her about assistance available from the Victim Crisis Assistance bureau and gives her his card, as well as one from the crisis bureau. He

o

tells the officer to give her a ride home. When the second patrol car gets back a few minutes later with the coffee.

The Primary Detective, Michael Cradle has now arrived. Cradle had trouble reaching the front gate of the White House because of the number of vehicles parked outside the house. There was mobile vans from local television stations, automobiles belonging to a variety of reporters, and two D.C. Metropolitan Police Department (MPD) squad cars, their uniformed occupants seated glumly inside them.

He flashed his MPD Detective badge at the Secret Service officer who left his guard post at the White House gate with German Shepherd in tow on a lease. The Secret Service officer flags him inside as the White House gate on North Portico side is opened. As he drives up in front of the White House, he noticed that the video surveillance camera was in place on the north portico.

He drives his car and parks it in the semi circular driveway. A large group of tourists assembled along the White House fence snapping pictures of each other with the White House as the perfect background. Also, a CNN reporter along with his cameraman is setting up shop in front of the Secret Service guard post to began late breaking cable television news. News has been leaked out from source inside of the White House about the murder of White House Counsel Richard Royster.

Michael Cradle is 31, 5'9, 165lbs, African-American man, who joined the D.C. Metropolitan Police Department (MPD) in 1986 and began investigating homicides as a MPD Detective in 1991. He has a B.A in Criminal Justice from Howard University. He'd had a clean record of seven years, a drawerful of citations of merit, letters from appreciative citizens and local politicians, no hint of being on the take, a good cop.

o

He actively lectures at local area colleges and universities in conjunction with the U.S. Attorney's Office of the District of Columbia as well as local high school youth leadership conferences.

He has been highly active in community service, leadership and mentoring African American youth since he was a teenage in the early 1980's. A proud alumni of Cardozo Senior High School Class of 1981. Currently, he remains a Homicide Detective and investigates high profile murders in his current assignment with the Major Case/Cold Case Squad.

Cradle get outs of his car, walks up to the White House, flashes his MPD detective badge to the two Marines dressed in Marine Dress Blues on each sides of the White House entrance door. He began viewing the crime scene carefully,he makes quick sketches of the locations of the major items in and around the body, while being extremely careful not to walk around too much or disturb anything unnecessarily. He obtains all of the pertinent information from the officer guarding the crime scene as to the victim's identity, age, height, weight, race etc., Then, he tells the Forensic crew to do their stuff.

They have already taken their general crime scene photos, so now one of them starts collecting evidence around the body, and placing it in bags, while the one acts as a scribe, and takes any additional photos that are necessary. This prevents all contamination of the team's cameras or notebooks from exposure to blood or other bodily fluids. Swabs of blood stains are taken.

Blood that is spattered on the wall is photographed with adhesive measuring tapes near it, for possible future "Blood Spatter Interpretation" by a forensic scientist. Samples of various fibers and materials from Richard Royster's office are taken and carefully labeled. The walls, desk and office furniture are carefully examined with a flashlight to check for bullet slugs that may have exited the body.

None are found, but if the autopsy shows a missing bullet, Royster's office will be torn apart to locate it. Anything that could conceivably be considered evidence is carefully bagged and labeled for future examination.

o

During this long and technical process, Michael Cradle and the Duty Sergeant have left the scene and goes back to the station The Forensic team telephones Cradle to ask if it is okay to remove the body from the crime scene.

Cradle says, "It is okay to remove the body, but to please photograph the back of Royster before placing him in the body bag."

Leaving instructions that the crime scene at the White House to be put under guard overnight with police tape across the door in the shape of an "X". They make their notes and go home as well.

The Forensic crew arrives back at the station, and placed the evidence in a biological storage room, carefully laying out any blood stained items on drying sheets. They make a few notes, put their film in the box for processing tomorrow, and call it a night. It is 4:10 a.m. As they are leaving, the Patrol Staff Sergeant tells them that the Chief Medical Examiner Bayes called to let them both and the detectives know that he had scheduled the autopsy for the next day at 1:00 p.m.

It's 9:00 a.m., and the Forensic crew meets with Cradle and his newly assigned partner for this investigation, in the Detective's office. The Staff Sergeant in charge of Detectives sits in on the meeting in the conference room, along with the Patrol Staff Sergeant, more out of curiosity than anything.

Cradle details the case so far, including the cooperative nature of the housekeeper. He reads out the history of Richard Royster, the victim. The Forensic crew reports that a generic test of the victim's clothes show stains that the stains are in fact blood.

The meeting is wrapped up for now. Cradle and his partner go out to have some lunch, before heading to the George Washington University Hospital(GWUH) for the autopsy.

In the GWUH morgue, they with the Chief Pathologist and his assistant, who are ready to start the post-mortem examination. The Forensic crew is already there, and have already photographed the body and seized Richard Royster's clothes as evidence. Overnight the body had been locked in a special freezer using a lock supplied by the D.C. Metropolitan Police Department, which is stored in the Detective's Office, to preserve evidence continuity.

The autopsy proceeds slowly, and every step is carefully documented by the Chief Pathologist John C. Beaird and his assistant. The Chief Pathologist Beaird takes his own photos in addition to the Forensic crew's and asks them to send him a copy of theirs as soon as they have them printed.

One of the Forensic officer asks if the pathologist feels that the wounds should be excised(cut out) for further examination by the crime lab if necessary, and the pathologist agrees that this is a good idea. The Chief Medical Examiner Bayes drops in to check on the progress of the investigation, asks the Pathologist when he would be willing to release the body to the family of Richard Royster. This matter being settled, he then leaves the room again.

Halfway through the autopsy a phone call comes for Michael Cradle that a car has been found. He tells the dispatcher that he would like another Forensic crew member to examine and photograph where it was found, and then tow it to the station evidence impound lot garage for further analysis.

The autopsy completed, the Chief Pathologist. Beaird states that the cause of death was a gunshot wound to the head, and that a total of three shots were fired, from a small caliber possibly a .38 pistol. All three slugs remain in the body, and the detectives and Forensic officers look at them closely. Although they are somewhat deformed, they all agree that they appear to be .38 slugs.

Leaving the autopsy at GWUH, the entire group of police personnel return to the station, where they are met by the other Forensic crew members. All law enforcement personnel have their work cut out for them at this point, doing literally reams of paperwork to complete the case.

o

Reports, court briefs, evidence lists, lab submission reports and crime scene logs all have to be completed by the Attorney General's Office. Dried evidence has to be properly labeled and stored, and evidence going to the crime laboratory has to be packaged and delivered, ensuring the continuity is never broken. Some evidence is examined in house before being stored.

The abandoned car is held for examination for two more days, and later is returned to the rightful owner. The car was impounded, but nothing significant to the investigation was found. The presence in the car of beer cans, an empty pack of cigarettes, wine bottle, and a corkscrew was the result of a trip to the beach by owner determined by the police investigation. Royster's wallet was in his Brooks Brother suit jacket and contained $4.98, credit cards, and miscellaneous papers, including the list of three psychiatrist provided by Deborah Hughes four days earlier.

Indeed, in the fury of activity surrounding the death of Richard Royster, Ashley Reid orders armed guards at Royster's office in a frantic attempt to remove the incriminating binders.

In addition to taking charge of the office, Ashley also made a call to the CIA around 10:40 p.m. EST, a strange call to make for a case involving the White House Counsel, reported Wilson, was an emergency number not be used for routine telephone calls.

The White House did not comply with D.C. Metropolitan Police Department requests that Richard Royster's office be immediately sealed off following his death. No ingress and egress by anyone other than the primary detective and his assistants was allowed at the crime scene at the White House.

The Looting of Royster's Office

o

Royster's office at the White House was being looted Secret Service agent Harold Hill watched as Ashley Reid's chief of staff Jennifer Thomas, carried several boxes of paper out of Richard Royster's office before D.C. Metropolitan Police officers showed up to properly seal it off from both inside and outside traffic.

Amazing when you consider that the official identification of Richard Royster's body by Larry Jones did not take place until 10 PM! Speaking of Larry Jones, another Secret Service agent saw him remove a lot of items from Richard Royster's office in direct violation of the official seal placed upon Royster's office. Witnesses also saw Matthew Greenbaum in Royster's office as well.

Three witnesses noted that Abraham Friesen, director of the White House Office of Administration, was desperate to find the combination to Richard Royster's safe. Mr. Friensen finally opened the safe, apparently with the help of a special"MIG" technical team signed into the White House in the late hours.

Two envelopes reported to be in the safe by Royster's secretary Linda Jones, addressed to Julie Holmes and to Robert Klein, were never seen again. When asked the next day regarding rumors of the safe opening, Michael Miller told reporters Royster's office did not even have a safe, a claim immediately shot down by former occupants of that office.

Later on that night, the D.C. Metropolitan Police officers arrived for the official search of Richard Royster's office, the police officers passively sit outside Royster's office as Greenbaum and Jones along with a bunch of White House aides freely went in and out of his office. Since Royster's office was technically part of the crime scene, this was a gross violation of police procedures.

A few White House aides were seen pilfering as well as ransacking Royster's office. A Secret Service agent saw Ruth Warren moving Royster's files to her office No efforts were made by D.C. Metropolitan Police to recover this potential evidence.

Why was this criminal interference with the police investigation tolerated?

o

A series of conflicts channeled from through Attorney General Jamie Woods Department of Justice resulted in the D.C. Metropolitan Police merely sitting outside Royster's office while Greenbaum continued his own search to Royster's office. During this search, he opened and upended Richard Royster's briefcase, showing it to be empty of its contents.

Royster's personal secretary, Linda Jones, has testified that Royster's file index, the document listing everything contained in his files, has vanished. Several other documents and letters, known by Jones to have been in Royster's wall safe, have also mysteriously vanished.

The documents removed from Royster's office at the White House and turned over to either the Reid's private attorney or the Royster's family attorney. According to one sole source, "This is ingenuous. For all we know, he may have seen only a handful innocuous documents. Furthermore, he makes no reference to the documents placed in the private living quarters of Ashley Reid.

The multitude of cardboard boxes full of documents removed from Royster's office by Ashley Reid's chief of staff, Jennifer Thomas, were taken to the private residence area of the White House! Eventually, only fifty four (54) pages emerged.

One set of billing records, under subpoena for two years, and thought to have been originated in Royster's office, turned up unexpectedly in the private quarters of the White House, with Ashley Reid's fingerprints all over them.

That proves that the blind trust documents were paramount importance to whoever directed the looting of Richard Royster's office. So, who ordered the looting of Richard Royster's office at the White House?

Which connects it to the murder.

o

President Thomas Jefferson Reid was unavailable at Camp David for the weekend. But Ashley Reid was on the telephone with someone at the White House in the moments before the looting took place.

The Washington Post headline read **"Richard Royster, White House Counsel Murdered"** on the morning of June 22, 1993. The news was sensational, feeding a frenzy lasting for several days, and investigation that may last years. The official story was Royster was clinically depressed, unable to survive in the big fish eat little fish world of Washington, DC, and was preparing to resign his position as White House Counsel to President Thomas Reid.

If Royster was depressed, he had good reasons to be as we shall see, none of which had to do with his personal life. His professional life--the secret side of it, on other hand, showed signs of unraveling at the seams, a very tangled web of intrigue and espionage.

According to William Webster, Royster was a senior intelligence officer working for the National Security Agency (NSA), holding the rank equivalent of general. Subsequent characterization by Edward Brown, one time senior editor at Forbes, described Royster as a key liaison between the White House, NSA, and Systematics-subsequently purchased by Systel--a company heavily involved in intelligence espionage. Somewhere between the two distinct profiles lays the real truth.

He was clearly involved in secretive intelligence work which certain powers wanted knowledge suppressed, in no small part because he was the homing beacon to their crimes and treachery.

Although Royster and Ashley made real sorts of dough with criminal money laundering deals reaching to the infamous BCCI scandal, it is Royster's alleged involvement with Israeli spy James Reynolds which give the most clues explaining his demise.

o

Prior to entering the White House, Royster, working in conjunction with British publishing magnate and former Member of Parliament, Maxwell Murdoch (1924-1991), had been identified as an espionage agent providing Israel highly classified information. Murdoch was found dead in his office in London, but was accorded a quasi state burial in Israel.

Much of Royster's espionage work concerned nuclear weapons and technology, with the ultimate goal of rendering Israel as a nuclear power in a gambit to deter its Arab neighbors from aggression.

Webster lays out a very persuasive case that Royster, who had begun work for the National Security Agency (NSA) around 1983, had been recruited by George Lincoln to act as his intermediary between Israeli spy James Reynolds who was ultimately convicted in 1988 of spying. The core mission of the NSA are to protect United States national security and to produce foreign signals intelligence information. The values of the NSA is to protect national security interests by adhering to highest standards of behavior.

But Royster was a jack of many tracks whose many talents would not be idled with just one project. He was involved in other NSA endeavors, including one which involved in financial spying and espionage.

Ironically, it was Royster's NSA project of tracking bank transactions using Inclaw's PREMIS software which may led to his downfall. One source alleges that a rogue CIA used the software to hack into JEMMAD's database where Royster's name was inexplicably found along with links to several Swiss bank accounts holding at various times up to 20 million dollars, which is not chump change for a Tennessee lawyer-even for one making $500,000 USD per year.

Ashley Reid had a direct interest in the money due to her many and varied collaborations with Royster in delicate financial matters. One of these banks was Banca della Svizzera Italiana (BSI). BSI is the oldest in the Swiss canton of Ticino. Founded in 1873 in Lugano as the **Banca della Svizzera Italiana**. Today BSI is an

o

institution that specializes in asset management and related services for private and institutional clients.

While this story of accidental discovery is plausible, we can consider it disinformation. It can be certainly believe that Royster had the accounts-why else would he make periodic day trips to Switzerland. But it is even likely this story was setup to paint Royster as a sinister traitor and to deflect attention away from his handlers who were the powers behind the treachery.

Ashley Reid: " Dick, I have something very serious to tell you."
Richard Royster: "What is it, you are trying to tell Ash?"
Ashley Reid: "Did you know your Swiss bank accounts have been drained through the use of surreptitious software."
Richard Royster: "Oh No!" "Say it is not so." (He is in total shock and his face is red)
Ashley Reid: "Yes it is true." Also, you are under investigation for treason and espionage."(An ignominy they share in common)
Richard Royster: "Damn!" "I am deep in doggy doo-doo."
Ashley Reid: "Dick, you need to go to Switzerland and check out for yourself."
Richard Reid: "Thanks Ash." (He gives her hug and walks away.)

On May 1, 1993, Royster bought a round trip an airline ticket from the White House Travel Office to Geneva in order to check-up on his Swiss bank accounts. Almost anyone can open a Swiss bank account, even US citizens are entitled to open an account and gain the advantages of financial security that comes with it. Switzerland is a politically, economically and geographically stable country which has built an entire industry based on this stability.

He discovered that his account of $2.8 million dollars had been emptied resulting in the hiring of legal counsel.

On May 18, he went to Maryland where he met with Jim Hubbell, William Cardozo and according to Laws, George Johnston among others including possible telephonic communications with the Reid's to strategies on damage control about

o

the money and reports to an explosive several should be confronted the illegality of his actions. Apparently, Hubbell showed Royster a printout of the money trail from JEMMAD to his Swiss bank accounts, a revelation which must surely conjured up substantial anxiety.

In the days preceding Royster's murder, two interesting events occurred which were most likely related to each other. The first according to Wilson is that the Democratic National Convention sent on June 16, a wire transfer in the amount of $295,000 via Shelly Farrell, to her sister-in-law Rebecca Royster, wife of Richard. Was this payola for Richard to keep his silence and perhaps console the loss of $2.8 million dollars USD from his Swiss bank account? Or was it hush money to Rebecca to keep her silence once Royster was dead? Who really the knows the answer?

We do know what Royster initially planned had to do something which Ralph Davis, a security man whom he conducted regular business, urged him not to do. Davis was gunned down gangland style a month later for knowing too much. The late Ralph Davis owned a detective agency in Nashville. According to Rose Davis, his widow, he had often done mysterious jobs for Richard Royster. She says that shortly before, he died, Royster telephoned Ralph. She overheard Ralph's half of the conversation. She says her husband became highly agitated. He begged Royster not to do something Royster was intent on doing. After Royster died, Ralph became extremely fearful and started carrying a gun. According to Rose, shortly thereafter, teams of Federal Bureau of Investigation (FBI) agents ransacked the Davis's house. They removed all boxes of office files, film negatives, and floppy disks. Rose says these searches happened repeatedly. The FBI thugs clearly indicating that all information was of the very highest order was a stake. Apparently, none of the searches or confiscations was legal.

In any event, Royster had overstepped his bounds and was permanently sequestered.

Royster had gotten in well over his head by taking possession of the nuclear launch codes which compromised the identification codes the President needed in order to initiate the launch of nuclear weapons. He was like a non swimmer literally drowning in the murky deep end of an information pool of files, records, declarations and blind trusts.

Royster had two 1 inch binders, one blue, one red, in the safe of Raymond Greenbaum. These binders were identified as NSA launch code and launch option books.

One disturbing aspect of this story is that Royster did not have clearance, even as a high rank NSA emissary, to see codes which are directly delivered to the President in his quarters. Thus the only way Royster could have obtained them is through Reid. Tom Reid was not the subject of espionage investigations; his wife was. We thus why she took charge of Royster's office immediately following his death. At this point, it is hard to know who gave the orders to murder Royster, but a good guess is that Hooks and Ashley closed ranks to silence him.

There is strong compelling evidence that Ashley and Royster were lovers but there are also intriguing tasty morsels about a White House lesbian clique with which Ashley may have been involved as well. It is one of the more reasonable claims made about the case in particular, although the credibility of these rumors is somewhat lessened by the fact that the people making the charge usually follow a few minutes later with a claim that Ashley was a lesbian. Who would questioned Ashley Reid's sexuality in the first place?

Carnegie Andrew Miller, the wealthy heir to the Miller publishing fortune was asked by the New York Times about his devotion to the Royster murder. Miller said "The death of Richard Royster: I think that's the Rosetta Stone to the whole Reid administration. There are just too many questions that have no answers."

Rebecca Royster arrived at the morgue at George Washington University Hospital (GWUH) to claim her husband's body dead on a cold slab. She is grief stricken at the sight of Richard being dead and cries profusely comforted by her sister-in-law.

o

Richard Royster body is picked up by a local mortuary and transported to their facility for embalming. Royster had requested his funeral to be held in Nashville, Tennessee.

That evening, at 8:30 p.m., Tom Reid was waiting to be interviewed by Larry King. As Reid was being prepped at Camp David by a makeup artist, he chatted with Mike Lewis. At 9:00 p.m., President Reid appeared via satellite from Camp David as a guest on CNN's "Larry King Live" to discuss the recent appointment of William Freeman to run the FBI and the Senate confirmation hearing of Jane Anderson Rosenberg to the United States Supreme Court.

Both developments had been well-received in the press and Reid was having such as good interview that King asked him to stay on past the scheduled show time. Yet there also had been victories early in the Reid administration but that was not a good reason to celebrate them at the moment.

Reid agreed, until John Watkins, Chief of Staff contacted the President at Camp David during the commercial break regarding the shooting death of Richard Royster.

President Reid's answered the call, a devastating look came on his face, learning of Royster's death in the White House. He later recalled. "Royster was overwhelmed, exhausted, and vulnerable to attacks by people who didn't play by the same rules he did."

President Reid, said " John, please call Rebecca Royster, Richard's spouse as soon as possible."

Watkins said, "I will call her Mr. President after our conversation Sir."

The call between the President and John Watkins ended. Now the sequences of events gets very interesting, say to least.

President Reid told his wife of the news of the murder of Richard Royster,

Tom Reid, said " Ashley, Dick Royster is dead, he was murder in his office at the White House."

Ashley Reid replied sobering with large tears in her eyes, " I am so sorry to hear of Dick's death Tom."

Tom Reid: "We are leaving now for Dick's house to comfort Rebecca and the kids."

Ashley Reid: "Okay Tom sounds like a plan to me in light of the current situation."

On the evening of June 21, President and First Lady left Camp David via Marine One traveling back to Washington, disembarking the helicopter to the waiting presidential limousine riding over to Royster's Georgetown home, The First Family arrived in a melancholic and saddened state to console his grieving wife Rebecca and children.

Reid recalled "sad for all my friends from Tennessee who had come to Washington wanting more than to serve and do good, only to find their every move second-guessed."

President Reid and First Lady Ashley Reid attended the funeral services along with Royster's immediate family consisting of his wife, Rebecca and two children: Jessica and Robert. Jessica was the oldest and she was a junior at Georgetown majoring in Sociology with Social and Criminal Justice emphasis. Robert was in the 12th grade, senior at St. Albans who enjoying playing lacrosse. Also, William Webster and Webster Kennedy attended the funeral as well.

President Reid gave the eulogy of his good boyhood friend Richard Royster. He described his good friend with humorous anecdotes in light of being a subdued and melancholy setting at the church.

Royster was born in Nashville, Tennessee on February 14, 1946, the same city as Tom Reid. It wasn't strange for the President to call Royster with offers to catch a movie, the men had know each other for years.

o

Kindergarten classmates, they only lived a few houses away from each other in Nashville, TN., before Reid's family had moved to Knoxville. Richard and Ashley were good friends. He joined the Hart Law Firm in Memphis and in 1973 was made a partner. Royster had recruited Ashley to join the firm after working with her on legal aid issues. Among his partners were Ashley Reid, William Bell and Webster Kennedy. Royster's office at the White House was located on the second floor of the West Wing which was a office suite. A few weeks after arriving he hired Linda Jones as his secretary.

Just a few weeks before Reid's Inauguration, Royster complained to his Memphis doctor that he was feeling down and anxious.

Royster's position as White House Counsel generally demanded that he work from between 7:30-8:30 a.m. in the morning until 9:30 p.m.or later, within six of seven days per week   The White House is an institution that never sleeps in direct comparison to New York City which is the city that never sleep. .During his first few months in Washington, Royster actively involved himself in most of the important pressing matters within the White House Counsel's office. At any given time there is at minimum thirty-one members (31) of staff working seemingly day and night in the White House.

 He took no vacation or weekends off until the weekend prior to his death. The demands of the White Counsel's office were severe, requiring him to be accomplishing a wide range of tasks in a short period of time. Royster had become a master juggler with his time and ultimate multi-tasker as well.

In the last six or eight weeks of his life those close to Royster observed that he appeared exhausted much of the time, his face appeared to be drawn and grey. He confide to some that he was having problems sleeping, and on certain morning commented that he had not slept at all.

Royster had a prescription for sleeping pills but did not want to take them for fear of becoming addicted. Although no one noticed a loss of appetite, it was obvious to many that he had lost weight. In last few weeks of his life Royster seemed

o

uncharacteristically fretful, and more quiet and subdued than usual. Family members noted that he had lost his sense of humor and appeared distracted.

Rebecca Royster described him as constantly worried and under stress. She believed that the White House Office of Communications matter was the single greatest cause of Royster's stress and anxiety in the weeks leading up to his death.

Linda Jones, Royster's secretary observed that spent much of the day on June 19, going through paperwork on his desk and in his desk drawers, dictating letters and taking care of unfinished business. She described Royster's day as one of "straightening and cleaning." Jones recalled that he spent much of the day with his office door closed.

Jones approximately six hours before his death, she recalls that at one point Royster came out of his office and placed three envelopes in the out-box on her desk for mailing out on that day. The envelopes had already been addressed and sealed by Royster, which was unusual thing for him. She looked at the envelopes to make sure they has postage and recalls that one was addressed to Royster's mother in Nashville, Tennessee, and another was addressed to an insurance company. She could not recall how the third envelope was addressed to. Deborah Hughes was with their mother when she received correspondence from Royster a day or two after his death. The letter contained oil leases which had been left to Royster's mother after his father died in 1990. Royster wrote a very brief typewritten cover letter providing instructions to his mother regarding the oil leases.
Rebecca Royster believes that the correspondence sent to the insurance company and the third envelope mailed by Royster were bill payments that she had asked him to make.

Linda Jones described Royster often as a "Southern Gentleman" with extremely genteel manners. He was especially courtly towards women. He seemingly had a healthy relationship with his mother. Despite this, his letter to his mother, sent only hours before he was murdered, does not contain a single expression. This is no hint whatsoever this would be his last communication with his mother.

On June 16, four days before his death, Royster showed up at the White House doctor's office, complaining that his heart was "pounding."

William Bell stopped by Royster's office on June 19, and Royster told him that the weekend had been good for him and that he and Rebecca were planning to go away the following weekend. Rebecca Royster recalls she and Royster had spoken about going away the following weekend but that no plans had been made as of later.

He told Bell, a close friend who at the time was serving as the Associate Attorney General, that no laws or rules of law had been broken but that in Washington you are assumed to have done something wrong even if you have not. He told Bell that he thought that the matter would never end. He became increasingly obsessed with the White House Office of Communications matter in the weeks before his death. Royster told Kennedy in connection with the Communications Office matter.

He told his sister Deborah Hughes, as well as his wife Rebecca, and his friend, Kennedy, that he was considering resigning from his position his position. Both Deborah Hughes and Rebecca Royster believed that personal humiliation, he would have felt had he returned to Tennessee under those circumstances prevented him from resigning.

Royster recommend that outside counsel be hired to represent the White House Counsel office in connection with the issues relating to the Communications Office firings. He was deeply disturbed by the Communications Office issues.
Royster had been Ashley's personal lawyer in Memphis, and he worried that he faced a serious conflict of interest. Royster began shopping around for his own lawyer, and frantically phoned Jack Peyton, an attorney located in Denver, Colorado, about the likelihood of Congressional hearing into the White House Office of Communications firings. Peyton who helped the Reid's fend off questions about Clearwater during the presidential campaign.

o

Royster's concerns that his role in the Communications Office matter might affect his objectivity in advising the Reid's. Peyton advise Royster, after reviewing the White House report, that he saw no conflict of interest.

On the morning of June 21, Peyton called the White House to confirm plans for a meeting with Royster the next day. But it was too late. Rather than return the call Royster left his office shortly for lunch and continued his busy work in his office several hours later.

During the particularly busy periods of late May and June, however, Royster was virtually involved.

Royster's friends and associates who knew him well, uniformly described him as man of honesty and integrity, respected for his intelligence and solid judgment. His professional reputation was of paramount importance to him, particularly among his colleagues in Tennessee.

Royster was characterized as quiet, reserved, and one who rarely showed anger or any emotion. Although difficult to get close to, he could be relied upon as a trusted and loyal confidante. Colleagues within the White House described him as a calming influence during stressful periods.

Royster's family and friends said that Royster did not experience any extended periods of depression prior to the spring of 1993. Although he experienced some brief episodes of depression and anxiety, these appeared to be resolved with medical treatment.

From time to time Royster experienced what his wife Rebecca described as anxiety or panic attacks, marked by heavy sweating and a strained voice. In late 1992, he told his primary physician in Memphis, Dr Harry Burns, that he was feeling depressed and anxious. At least two of Royster's closest relatives have suffered from periods of depression.

o

Royster remained at the firm until January 1993, when he moved to Washington, D.C. to assume the position as White House Counsel. At the same time, Kennedy joined the White House Counsel's office and Bell became Associate Attorney General.

One of the small cadre of disciples who followed the Reid's from Tennessee to Washington, D.C in 1992. Royster settled in as White House Counsel, a powerful position in which he interfaced with Ashley Reid daily. He wasn't use to the intensity of the work pace and the relentlessness of the political foes of the new administration.

Royster nicknamed "Stretch" for his tall skinny, lanky frame, has mastered the legal environs in Memphis as a partner in the Hart Law Firm. He had been very happy there, with time leftover to spend with his family and serve local charitable causes. But the Capital beltway is long way home from the country roads and tree lined streets of Tennessee.

Then he came from the little known and even less understood southern locale as a hand picked member of Reid's governing team seems to have spurred the conservative Wall Street Journal editorial board to write four editorials in May and June. These editorials questioning Royster's adherence to the rule of law, ethics and even his identity, as the White House Office of Communications had refused to release a photo of the new White House Counsel.

Richard Royster was a Tennessee lawyer which would invoked the visions of Mayberry RFD and apple pies cooling in the window sill. An imputation of a happy overstuffed, slow paced life in the south and satisfactory lived but long to be forgotten in time. An era frozen in time and memory.

But the phrase "Tennessee Lawyer" took a sharp turn to the dark side during the 1990s, and Royster was dragged effortlessly along with it.

o

A private burial was to be held at the Royster family crypt at the Heavenly Acres Cemetery in Nashville. Royster's father Joseph was also interred there after he died of cancer three years ago.

Ashley Reid was deeply saddened by the untimely death of Richard Royster, she became depressed after the funeral was over, refusing even to get out of bed to carry out her official duties as First Lady for several days. She had her Chief of Staff to cancel her appointments due to the mourning period for Dick Royster.

TIMELINE
14 Feb 1946   Dick Royster born, Nashville, TN
         1962   Graduates Osborne High School
         1966   Graduates Wilkinson College
         1969   University of Tennessee School of Law, first in his class
         1970   Married Rebecca Bailey
Jan 1993 Royster accepts a position as White House Counsel for the Reid Administration
21 June 1993 Royster attends a Rose Garden ceremony to announce William Freeman as FBI chief
21 June 1993 Dick Royster murdered at White House with a .38 revolver
21 June 1993 At 8:48 pm, Chief Medical Examiner confirms Royster's death
22 June 1993 Chief Pathologist conducts an autopsy at George Washington University Hospital

Three days after Richard Royster's murder, the much delayed trust declarations were delivered to the trustee's office.

The paperwork carried Royster's signature. Whoever completed the papers remains an absolute mystery, but one thing's very clear here. The paperwork and records for the blind trust had to have been among the dozen boxes of records looted from Richard Royster's office prior to its being sealed properly off by the investigating officers.

However, some inconsistencies have led many conspiracy theorists to suggest why Richard Royster was murdered, presumably to prevent him from revealing some deep dark secrets about one or both of the Reid's. A really interesting and intriguing proposition to be pondered in the inquiring mind of our great detective.

Detective Michael Cradle has his investigative work cut out for him. The real work began now to find out who, what, why and how Richard Royster was murdered.

o

The long enduring process of conducting an investigation is the tall order for Cradle to be carried out. He has the experience, competency and ability to take on the task with much enthusiasm and eagerness to get the job done right..

CHAPTER TWO
THE INVESTIGATION

> Oh what a tangled web to weave, When first we practise to deceive!
> Sir Walter Scott, Marmion, Canto vi. Stanza 17
> Scottish author & novelist (1771-1832)

The Federal Bureau of Investigation (FBI) would have had the primary investigative jurisdiction if the circumstances fell within the Presidential and the Presidential Staff statute, Title 18, United States Code, Section 1751. The statute makes it a federal crime to, among other things, kill the President, Vice President, or a specified number of persons appointed by the President or Vice President.

The statute further provides that violations shall be investigated by the FBI. 18 U.S.C. Section 1751 covers "any person appointed under section 105 (a) (2) (A) of title 3 employed in the Executive Office of the President..."Title 3, United States Code, Section 105 (a) (2) (A) provides that the President may appoint twenty-five employees at a specified rate of pay. Because the preliminary investigation by the FBI provided no indication of criminal activity, the FBI did not determine whether or not Royster was covered by this statute. The FBI's inquiry into this matter was closed

The D.C. Metropolitan Police Department (MPD) was immediately assigned to the investigation. Normally an investigation into the violent death of one of the highest officers of the federal government is handled by the FBI. However, it now seems clear the entire time the MPD worked on the case, the FBI was secretly involved. Did the White House direct this subterfuge? If so, for what purpose?

Cradle obtained telephone records from the White House reflects that in the early afternoon of June 16, Royster made two calls to one of psychiatrists recommended by his sister. At 12:41 p.m. and again at 1:24 p.m., Royster called the psychiatrist from the telephone in his office, and charged the calls to his home phone. Each call lasted one minute or less. Calls of less than one minute are reflected on a telephone bill as one minute in length.

The psychiatrist called by Royster often uses an answering machine during the lunch hour when no one is in the office. It is possible that Royster reached the answering machine and did not attempt to leave a message. Neither the psychiatrist that Royster attempted to reach nor the other psychiatrist recommended by Deborah Hughes ever spoke to Royster.

However, the list of psychiatrists was found on a handwritten piece of paper inn Royster''s wallet following his death. Royster told Deborah during a telephone conversation on June 19 that the weekend had gone well,and he was contemplated getting away more often.

He also said that he was not yet ready to contact a psychiatrist. On the same date, Royster contacted Dr. Harry Burns, his personal physician. He told Burns that he was under a great deal of stress and was depressed. Burns prescribed an antidepressant drug called Desyrel, which has the generic name trazadone. Burns stated that he had never before prescribed an antidepressant for Royster.

A CVS pharmacy in Washington filled the prescription for thirty (30) tablets, a dosage of 50 milligrams per tablet, and had the tablets delivered to Royster's Georgetown home in the late afternoon on July 19. The pharmacy had no previous record of having filed any prior prescription for Royster. Rebecca Royster saw Royster take one tablet during that evening. Royster left work earlier than usual that particular day and arrived home around 7:45 p.m.

During the evening Royster received a call from President Reid. The President had heard from White House staff that Royster was feeling down about the White House Office of Communications matter and called to invite Royster to watch a movie with him and others at the White House theater.

Royster politely declined the President's invitation. After chatting about Royster's weekend in Maryland, the President told him that he wanted Royster's advice on making some possible White House organizational changes. They agreed to meet on Friday, June 21. The President did not perceive during the conversation that Royster was downcast or depressed at the time.

o

The main investigation is being led by Detective Michael Cradle who received a call from the Duty Sergeant about the car which was discovered parked outside the White House during the crime scene, was a vehicle from a Capitol Hill dentist reported stolen, several weeks ago from her parking space behind her office. The car was impounded and searched, but nothing significant to the investigation was found.

During that he was depressed, he asked her to recommend a place he and his wife Rebecca could go to relax for the weekend. She called Rebecca Royster with two bed and breakfast inns located on Maryland's picturesque Eastern Shore near Ocean City. Before they left, Royster told his wife that he was depressed, and she could tell that he was still under same telephone call in which Royster told his sister Deborah Hughes that he was under great stress while they were driving through various cities in Maryland.

Coincidentally, William Bell and his wife were also on the Eastern Shore of Maryland for the weekend staying with friends, Michael and Carolyn Cardozo in their two (2) bedroom condominium timeshare, who also knew the Roysters.

On Saturday, June 17, the Cardozo's invited the Royster's over to their home, and the group spent Saturday evening and Sunday together. Bell described it as a relaxing weekend during which Royster jogged, went boating, hit some golf balls, read the newspaper, and ate some fresh Maryland Blue Crabs for the very first time. Royster and Bell spoke about the need to change their lifestyles and spend more time away from work. Royster mentioned that he missed spending more time away from work during the summer months of June and July at his vacation home in city of North Muskegon, Michigan, as he had while at the Hart Law Firm.

Somewhat in contrast to Bell's perception of the weekend, Rebecca Royster stated that the weekend did not go particularly well for Royster. When Royster returned on Sunday, June 18, he spoke to Weaver by telephone. They discussed the White House office of Communications matter for approximately thirty (30) minutes in

o

detail and that they would plan to meet face-to-face in Washington to further discussed it further on June 21.

Next, Detective Cradle decides to re interview the White House housekeeper, Anna Chavez, who was first to discover the dead body of Richard Royster in his office at the White House . He schedules the interview to take place promptly at twelve noon on July 1st. The White House's housekeeper's work shift does not start until 4:00 pm. in the White House Facilities and Maintenance Department.

Meanwhile, he reviews the report of the housekeeper typewritten by the first patrol officer who arrived at the crime scene at the White House for any inconsistencies in her version of the story. At the onset there is no new leads currently in the case to build from. Cradle contacts his assistant to obtain the Pathologist report who performed the autopsy at the George Washington Hospital several weeks ago on Richard Royster. A few days passed until the Pathologist's Report is received in Cradle's office at D.C. Metropolitan Police Headquarters.

The housekeeper manages to arrive at Cradle's office at 12:30 pm on July 1 as oppose twelve noon. She had called a taxicab to pick her up since her car would not start. The taxi pulls up at Metropolitan Police Department headquarters on 300 C Street NW. She is screened by security and passes through the metal detector and proceeds to take the elevator to Detective Michael Cradle's office is located on the fifth floor. Cradle's office is numbered 525. She enters his office door where Cradle cheerfully greets her and shakes her hand with a firm grip.

The face-to-face interview with the White House housekeeper promptly begins:

Cradle: "Please state your name?"
Housekeeper: My name is "Anna Chavez"
Cradle: "How long have you worked as a housekeeper at the White House"
Chavez: " I have worked there for ten years."
Cradle: "What time did you discover Richard Royster's body"
Chavez: "I had just started my shift two hours ago, when I walked into Richard Royster's office to clean and pick-up the trash, It was 6 pm.

o

Cradle: " Where was the body found?"
Chavez: " I found him slumped down over at his desk faced down."
Cradle: "Did you any see blood stains?"
Chavez: "Yes, I saw his blood splatter on the desk and white shirt stained."
Cradle: "Had the office been looted when you first discovered the body.""
Chavez: "No, the office was full of paper scattered on his desk and several boxes on the floor.
Cradle: "What did you do after you discovered his body?"
Chavez: " I called my supervisor."
Cradle: " Did you see anyone else enter the office after you called your supervisor."
Chavez: "No"
Cradle: " I have no further questions at this time." "Is there anything do you think I have left out."
Chavez: "No."
Cradle: "Thank you for your time, speaking with me today."

The interview is completed but no new surprising or shocking information to be disclosed. The housekeeper's story is consistent with the details in the patrol officer's incident report that Cradle read previously.

Now ,a mysterious letter shows up at Cradle's office, after the housekeeper Anna Chavez has left Cradle's office enroute to catch the elevator back downstairs. Cradle takes the precaution of putting on a pair of plastic clothes to preserve the letter for testing by the forensic lab.

The letter is handwritten on White House stationery dated June 25, 1993 which read as follows:

Dear Det. Michael Cradle:
 Mistakes was made from ignorance, inexperience and overwork;
No one in the White House, to my knowledge, violated any law or standard of conduct.
There was no intent to benefit any individual or specific group by committing the murder.
The press is covering up the illegal benefits.
Catch me if you can!

o

Leave me alone.
Back off!!

Signed,
X Assassin Executor

Michael Cradle suddenly drew a puzzled on his face upon reading the mysterious letter he had received. Who sent this letter? Why? To further complicate the matter the ink on the letter appears to be fading out. So Cradle immediately have the letter sealed in an evidence bag and sent to the crime lab across town via courier for evaluation by forensic scientists.

Cradle looks down at his watch and see that is now four o'clock and he has to leave his office to go over to the Boys & Girl Club Capitol Hill Branch to speak to a group of aspiring young boys and girls who he regularly mentors at the facility.

The mysterious letter has now arrived at the Metropolitan Police Department (MPD) crime laboratory. One of the forensic scientist on duty removes the letter from the marked evidence bag. The letter is in placed a solution to preserve the contents from disappearing from sight, so it can be photographed by his assistant.

An handwriting analysis performed by the MPD laboratory could not confirm the identity of the author of the letter.

Now, the letter has finally stop fading out and disappearing from sight. It is placed in another type of evidence bag for filing and cataloging in the evidence archival system.

The forensic scientist completes the evidence reporting the finding of his evaluation of the letter, a copy to be send to Detective Cradle by tomorrow morning. At least the letter was not lost forever due to the disappearing ink that was it written in.

A really strange twist is the use of White House stationery being used a strange person or party who hand writes as oppose to using a computer with a word

o

processor application such Microsoft Word to compose it such a letter. An extremely puzzling situation.

Detective Cradle arrives back at his office to find the forensic scientist evidence findings report on his desk. He promptly reads it to see who may have written it, the Forensic scientist concludes the letter was written in invisible ink by an unknown author. The mysterious letter is important in one way but inconsequential in the other.

Cradle is furious that the mysterious letter is just that a mysterious piece of documentary evidence. He fumes out of his office into the Chief's office and proceeds on breaking the facsimile machine on the desk.

Then, he catches the elevator downstairs and walks out of the door to get a Latte at the Starbucks down the street across from the D.C. Superior Courthouse. Cradle orders his a Mocha Frappuccino and takes a seat at the window.

He stares out in space, closes his eyes begin reflecting on the events of the day and from the past three weeks from the time of Richard Royster's death at the White House.

Cradle is thinking to himself that this murder case will possibly go down as an unsolved one. No real suspect is hunted down, arrested and brought to justice. A case of this magnitude be heart-breaking for a homicide detective of Cradle's caliber but that is the nature of the beast and the job itself.

This is the reason that Cradle has managed to be a top detective in the department and an exemplar of what good detective is to a lot of rookies who he mentor down through the years. A passion for excellence in his duty to serve and protect the citizenry of Washington, DC.

The following day, Cradle tells his Chief that he broke his fax machine.
Cradle: "Chief, I have something to tell you."
Chief: "What do you have to tell me Michael?"

o

Cradle: "I broke your fax machine on yesterday."
Chief: "I am surprised at you breaking my fax machine in my office."
Cradle: "I did it because I was upset with the way the Royster murder case was unfolding.'
Chief: "You are my top detective in this department and I do understand how much a perfectionist you are with these murder cases."
Cradle: " I am very sorry Chief, I would not let it happen again."
Chief: "Okay Michael, next time go to the gym and punch the bag instead."
Cradle: "Alright Chief, I will."

At the time of the autopsy, there are a total of four gunshots to the head and torso. The sequence of the infliction cannot be determined for certain and is therefore arbitrarily labeled in the report. The following day Cradle received the report from the Pathologist's office.
Cradle began to read it as follows:

I hereby certify that I, John C. Beaird, M.D. have performed an autopsy on the body of Richard Royster on the 22nd day of June, 1993 at 1:00 p.m. in Washington, D.C. at George Washington University Hospital.

The purpose of this report is to provide a **certified opinion** to the Washington,D.C. Chief Medical Examiner and District of Columbia Attorney General. The facts and findings to support these conclusions are filed with the District of Columbia Department of Health.

EXTERNAL EXAMINATION

The body is that of an adult white male measuring 72 ½ inches and weighing 197 pounds. The body is normally developed and appears consistent with the given age

o

of 47 years. He is received with white shirt, white undershirt, navy blue suit, red striped tie, black belt, white boxer shorts, two black socks and 2 black shoes. All the clothing is stained with blood. The shirt have defects consistent with gunshots wounds to the body. Post mortem changes consist of fixed posterior livor mortis and full rigor mortis.

The scalp hair is mixed gray, wavy and short. The corneas are cloudy. The sclerae and conjunctivae are unremarkable. No discrete petechiae be present. The irides are blue. The mouth contains natural teeth. There is no mustache and beard present. The palate and frenula are intact. The ears, nose and mouth show no abnormalities. The neck is of normal configuration and there is no palpable masses. The thorax is symmetrical. The abdomen is flat. The axilla, external genitalia, and anus are without trauma. The extremities are symmetrical and normally developed.

No identifying marks such as a tattoo is present. There are no scars on the abdomen, back and on the extremities.

There is no evidence of emergency medical intervention.

EVIDENCE OF INJURY: At the time of the autopsy, there are a total of four gunshots wounds to the head and torso. The sequence of the infliction cannot be determined for certain and is therefore arbitrarily labeled in the report.

The autopsy found a bullet entered the cranial cavity, significantly damaging the left side of the brainstem and the left cerebral hemisphere of the brain, and exited from the center of the back of the head.

There is a 3/16 inch close range penetrating wound on the right temple, at 3 inches below the top of the head and 4 inches right of the anterior midline. There is a zone of soot around the entrance wound which measures 1 inch x ¾ inch in greatest dimension.

o

A hemorrhage wound track passes leftward, backward, and downward causing patchy subscalpular, patchy skull fractures, patchy hemorrhage, patchy subarachnoid hemorrhage, extensive damage to the bases of the right frontal and temporal lobes, left temporal lobe, and a distorted copper jacketed and medium caliber bullet is lodged and recovered inside the left area canal.

There is a 5/16 inch diameter diameter distant wound on the right side of the chest, at 17 ½ inches below the top of the head and 4 ½ inches right side of the anterior midline. There is a marginal abrasion noted around the entrance wound which measures ½ inch in diameter. There is no evidence of soot material or powder tattooing appreciated in around the entrance wound. A hemorrhagic wound track passess backward, downward, and leftward through the right anterior 4th intercostal space, with perforation to the middle lobe of the right lung, right lobe of the liver, right posterior 11th intercostal space, and the bullet and ¾ inches right of the posterior midline, with the exit wound measuring ¼ inch in diameter. There is approximately 750 mL of blood inside the right chest cavity.

There is a ¼ inch diameter distant perforating gunshot wound on the left side of the chest, at 21 inches below the top of the head and 3 inches left of the anterior midline. There is a marginal abrasion noted around noted around the entrance wound with one at 12 o'clock position measuring ⅛ inch in thickness and one at the 6 o'clock position measuring 3/16 inch in thickness. There is no evidence of soot material or powder tattooing appreciated in around entrance wound.

A hemorrhagic wound track passess backward and slightly downward through the left anterior 6th rib cartilage with perforation to the left lobe of the liver, stomach, pancreas in two halves, left kidney, left posterior 11th intercostal space, and the bullet exits through the left side of the back, at 23 ¾ inches below the top of the head and 3 inches left of posterior midline, with the exit wound measuring ¼ inch in diameter, There is approximately 50 mL of blood inside the abdominal.

There is another 5/16 inch diameter distant perforating gunshot wound in the middle of the chest, at 17 ½ inch below the top of the head and 4 ½ inches middle of the anterior midline. There is a marginal abrasion noted around the entrance

o

wound measures ½ inch in diameter. There is no evidence of soot material or powder tattooing appreciated in or around the entrance wound.

A hemorrhagic wound track passes backward, downward, and leftward through the right anterior 4th intercostal space with perforation to the middle lobe of the right lobe of the liver, right posterior 11th intercostal space, and the bullet exits through the middle of the back, at 25 ¼ inches below the top of the head and 1 ¾ inches right of the posterior midline, with the exit wound at ensuring ¼ inch in diameter. There is approximately 375 mL of blood inside the middle chest cavity.

INTERNAL EXAMINATION

HEAD AND NECK: The brain weighed 1230 grams. There is no epidural hemorrhage. The vasculature overlying the cerebral hemispheres is congested. The structures at the base of the brain, including cranial nerves and large vessels, are intact, except for the injuries described. Serial sections through the cerebral hemispheres, cerebellum, and brain stem reveal no tumor or evidence of infection.

The neck is without soft tissue hemorrhage or palpable and the structures surrounding the upper airway are intact. Sections through the thyroid gland and tongue are unremarkable.

CARDIOVASCULAR SYSTEM: The heart weighed 360 grams. The epicardium is intact and smooth. The coronary arteries arise from unobstructed ostia, follow the usual distributions, and are without significant arteriosclerosis. The cardiac valves are normally formed and chambers of usual dimensions. The atrial and ventricular are intact. The myocardium is red-brown firm and unremarkable. The aorta and its major branches are intact.

RESPIRATORY SYSTEM: The right lung weighed 340 grams and the left 640 grams. The pulmonary arteries are without thromboemboli on initial incision into the pulmonary trunk and on dissection. On sectioning the pulmonary parenchyma is mildly to moderately congested, edematous, and without focal lesions.

DIGESTIVE SYSTEM AND LIVER: The esophagus is unremarkable with a sharp gastroesophageal junction. The unremarkable stomach is full. The duodenum, small intestines, appendix, and large intestine are unremarkable. The liver weighed 1920 grams.
The parenchyma is red-brown and soft without focal lesions. The unremarkable gallbladder contains approximately 11 cc of bile. The extrahepatic bile ducts are patent and unremarkable. The pancreas is otherwise unremarkable.

RETICULOENDOTHELIAL SYSTEM: The spleen weighed 170 grams. There is a normal distribution of unremarkable lymph nodes. The thymus gland is unremarkable.

GENITOURINARY SYSTEM: The right and left kidney weighed 150 grams and 170 grams, respectively. The subcapsular surfaces are smooth. The cortices are of normal thickness with sharp corticomedullary junctions. The calyces, pelves, and ureters are patent and unremarkable. The unremarkable urinary bladder contains approximately 725 cc of urine.

Serial sections of the bilateral testes reveal no evidence of trauma. Serial sections of the prostate demonstrate no gross abnormality.

ENDOCRINE SYSTEM: The pituitary, thyroid, parathyroid, and adrenal glands are unremarkable.

MUSCULOSKELETAL SYSTEM: The musculoskeletal system is unremarkable.

TOXICOLOGY: The following specimens were submitted for possible toxicological analysis: blood, bile, and vitreous humor.

No alcohol or drugs found in Royster's blood, although a later analysis by the FBI lab revealed small traces of trazodone, attributable to the antidepressant prescribed by Dr. Jones, Royster primary physician

Photographs taken during the autopsy by the Forensic crew, as well as microscopic slides of tissues from Dr. Beaird and reviewed by the Pathologist Panel.

Dr. Beaird certified the death as homicide.the office's x-ray machine was operable at the time of Royster's autopsy, and as a result x-rays were taken as well.

The lab conducted tests on the blood sample obtained during Royster's autopsy. The tests revealed small concentrations of trazadone, diazepam and nordiazepam. Trazodone is the antidepressant prescribed by Dr. Jones and taken by Royster on the evening of June 19.

Diazepam is commonly as valium, and nordiazepam is a metabolite of valium. The concentrations of these drugs were below generally recognized therapeutic levels. Royster's blood type was found to be consistent with blood found on his shirt and undershirt.

Finally, the Panel was provided with summaries of interviews with Royster's family and friends during which they described Royster's depressed state prior to his death.

The Pathologist Report states that information that Royster took an antidepressant prior to his death, which corroborated by the findings of a trace of trazadone, antidepressant, identified in Royster's blood.

The lab conducted an analysis of the blood staining on Royster's face and clothing as depicted in the photographs taken at the scene. The photograph show Royster's face pointing straight up-his head not tipped to either side. This position is inconsistent with the blood patterns on Royster's face and shirt.

The blood on the right shoulder of Royster's shirt-consisting of saturating stains of having been caused by a flow of blood onto soaking into the fabric.

The blood on Royster's right right cheek and jaw is a contact blood stain, typical of having been caused by a blotting action, such as would happen if a blood soaked

o

object was brought in contact with the side of his face and taken away, leaving the observed pattern.

Polaroid and 35 mm photographs were taken of the body and the office area containing two office chairs, sitting sofa and coffee table, however clearly depict the condition of Royster's body shortly after the arrival of Metropolitan Police Department.

The photographs show blood stains on Royster's face and on the right shoulder of his shirt. The staining of his shirt covered the top of his shoulder from his neck to the upper arm. The photographs of his face show two lines of blood, one running from the right corner of his mouth to below the right ear, and the other from the right nostril toward the temple above the right ear.

The photographs also show a larger area of blood staining Royster's right cheek and jaw, forming what is described in the lab report as a "contact stain."

The lab concluded that the pattern of the blood on Royster's face and on Royster's shoulder is consistent with Royster's face having come in contact with the shoulder of his shirt at some point. Because Royster's head in not in contact with his shoulder in the photographs, the lab reports concludes that Royster's head moved or was moved after being in shoulder.

The Pathologist Panel endorsed this conclusion, stating that "a rightward tilt of his face was changed to a forward orientation by one of the observers before the scene photographs were taken."

The lab also found extensive blood staining on Royster's shirt and undershirt, covering a vastly greater amount of his shirt then that was depicted in the photographs : taken at the scene. This staining is attributable to the movement of the body from the scene, which is typically results in additional staining of the deceased's clothing. After Royster's body was placed into the body bag and his body laid flat, some of the blood that settled in the lower part of his body then flowed out, causing significant additional blood staining on his clothes and face.

o

The lab also conducted DNA analysis on material from an area within 5cm of Royster's shirt.

This DNA was compared to the DNA in Royster's blood, and the lab found it to be exactly the same type. This DNA type is shared among approximately six (6) percent of Caucasians in the world.

This material is derived from a cellular material, most likely blood or saliva. the lab examined the pair of prescription eyeglasses found lying on Royster's desk and compared them to his optical prescriptions provided by Rebecca Royster.
The forensic crime laboratory found that the prescriptions were consistent with the determined prescriptions of the eyeglasses found on Royster's desk in the White House.

The marks on the earpieces were found to be consistent with biting. Rebecca Royster stated that Royster had a habit of biting the earpieces of his glasses. The lab determined that Royster's clothing contained head hairs similar to his own.

The Pathologist stated that the precise time of Richard Royster's death was 6:00 p.m. on June 21, 1993.

The organs occupy normal positions, and all the internal organs are in a state of autolysis. There are no adhesions or mass lesions.

In addition, the Pathologist Panel discussed the evidence with the members of the Detective's office, the investigating officers, and the lab personnel.

In order to test the veracity of the information provided by the Metropolitan Police Department (MPD), the Pathologist office performed a detailed analysis of that information. MPD provided the details include specific information by the housekeeper who discovered Royster's body and the location of the body in his White House office.

o

Two members of the Panel met with the Chief Medical Examiner Dr. Bayes. After reviewing and analyzing the evidence, the Pathologist Panel issued a report stating its conclusions and summarizing the bases for its conclusions.

The Panel concluded the following:

1) The bullet wound to Royster's head and brain caused his death;
2) The bullet traveled and entered the cranial cavity significantly damaged the left side of the brainstem and the left cerebral hemisphere of the brain and exited from the center of the back of the head;
3) The wound caused instantaneous complete incapacitation, followed by clinical death within a matter of minutes;
4) Two bullets in the chest cavity and lodged there in ensured the victim was dead.
5) Royster was murdered where he was found in his office in the White House.

This 47 year white male was discovered deceased slumped over on his desk with multiple gunshot wounds to the body on June 21, 1993. EMS responded to the crime scene to confirm asystole. An autopsy was performed on June 22, 1993.

Major autopsy findings include a total of four gunshot wounds to the body with one close range penetrating wound to the right temple, and three distant perforating gunshot wounds to the torso, with injuries to the brain, left eye, right lung, liver, stomach, pancreas, and left kidney, resulting in right hemothorax and hemoperitoneum.

The Pathologist Report does not purport to provide definitive answers to all questions surround Richard Royster's death. The overwhelming weight of the evidence compels that Royster was murdered. Although the contributing factors to his depressed state can never be precisely determined, there is no evidence that any issues to the Presidential Blind Trust and White House Office of Communications matter played any part in his murder.

o

Pathologist Report states that these conclusions were arrived at separately and independently by each member of the Panel.
Electronically signed by John C. Beaird, M.D. on Saturday 22, 1993 Chief Pathologist.

The Pathologist Report was accurate and conclusive to the point on how Richard Royster was murdered at the White House by the infliction of multiple gunshots to the body.

Cradle had requested telephone call logs from the White House Office of Communications that he received via special courier service over at police headquarters. The night before Royster's death, the President called and asked him if he'd like to come over to watch a movie--In the Line of Fire, with Clint Eastwood. "No thanks," Royster said, "I'm already home with Rebecca, and I don't think I should head back to the White House."

President Reid said he called Royster that Thursday night to speak to his friend, whom he missed. Ashley Reid made a tear filled call to several of her staff members who all have known Royster for years. Like everyone around him. Also, Ashley placed at call to the CIA around 10:40 p.m.which was scrambled and the telephone call log appeared sketchy as best.

Ashley said she never thought Richard Royster would be a victim of murder. "Of a thousand people, of those who might be murdered. I would never pick Dick in a thousands years " she later told a reporter from the Atlantic Reporter magazine.

Yet more than Tom Reid, it was Dick Royster's relationship with Ashley that fueled many of the persistent theories surround his death. The rumors of an affair between Royster and Ashley, a persistent allegation that dogged them both since since their days in Memphis. Reid would speak to Royster again the next day at the Rose Garden ceremony, the last time he'd see his friend alive again.

o

Problems surfaced right away for our primary investigator namely Michael Cradle attempting to keep the Royster narrative straightforward as the recollections of Pathologist Panel, emergency response personnel, and patrol police arriving on the crime scene at the White House.

With the high profile nature of Royster's death must come many high profile investigations into it. Royster was murdered matching the conclusions of the Metropolitan Police Department, Detective Michael Cradle, Chief Medical Examiner, Chief Pathologist, and the FBI crime lab.

Royster's family seeks end to the theories of his demise. The facts they with all certainty are certainly grim enough. Royster's family deserve to have some closure and definite answers for reasons he was murdered.

Now the manhunt for the killer was officially on!

o

CHAPTER THREE
THE SEARCH IS ON

" I could be blindfolded and dropped into the deepest ocean and I would know where to find you. I could be buried a hundred miles underground and I would know where you are."
Neil Gaiman, American Gods(American Gods, #1)

o

Now the marathon of the search is on for the murder of Richard Royster who is a mysterious shadowing dark figure on the radar screen of one sharp detective Michael Cradle. The search for the killer is intensifying since almost a month has past since he received the Pathologist Report which concluded it as a homicide by multiple gunshots wounds to Royster's head and body.

Washington, D.C. is a spectacular place to celebrate July 4! The National Mall with the Washington DC's monuments and the U.S. Capitol in the background, forms a beautiful and patriotic backdrop to America's Independence Day celebrations. Public access to the National Mall begins at 10:00 a.m., with all visitors required to enter via a security checkpoint. This is all day event in the nation's capitol, beginning with a parade along Constitution Avenue and ending with a spectacular display of fireworks over the Washington Monument.

The 4th of July celebrations in Washington, DC are the most attended events of the year. Many people arrive early including Detective Michael Cradle along with his daughter and son to stake out a good seat on the lawn. Even Cradle deserves some needed time off from investigative police work to enjoy "Capitol Fourth 1993" live and in person with his family. The 1993 Independence Day concert is telecast live at 8:00 p.m. ET from the lawn of the U.S. Capitol in Washington, DC on Public Broadcasting Service (PBS), hosted by E.G. Marshall along with Johnny Cash, June Cash, Mary Chapin Carpenter, Rita Moreno, Peter Nero, Erich Kunzel, National Symphony Orchestra (NSO), Singing Sergeants of the US Air Force and the US Army Chorus. The show culminates with the NSO playing the War of 1812 Overture, cannons firing and fireworks bursting in air. A spectacular light show in the Washington, D.C. skies on a hot fourth of July night.

The D.C. Metropolitan Police Department had posted a phone number for leads in the case on their website, both Metro and Metro Bus billboards and signs throughout the area. In addition to the Crimestoppers reward, the family offered twenty five thousands dollars($25,000) for information leading to an arrest.

Call MPD police at 202-727-5000 or Crimestoppers at 202-355-TIPS.

o

However, no mug shot to be posted on America's Most Wanted television program at this juncture of the case.

The search trail had gone cold for the moment investigating the violent murder in the capitol city of Washington, D.C. The search for the killer in the Richard Royster tragedy continues on this 5 day of July 1993 and there are new developments in the case. Cradle received anonymous tip from a caller who saw the tip line phone number posted on billboards in Metro subway stations throughout the extensive transportation system.

Caller: "I saw a man dressed. as a Secret Service agent running through Lafayette Park across the street from the White House at around 6:15 pm on June 21, 1993."
Cradle: "Could you see his face?"
Caller: "He wore a black ski mask covering his face."
Cradle: "Do you think that it is kind of a strange for him to wearing a ski mask in summer."
Caller: "Yes"
Cradle: "Did you see him leave the park?"
Caller: "Yes, he left the park and got into a black suburban parked on Eye Street."
Cradle: "Could you make out the license plate on the vehicle."
Caller: "No the plate was covered and blocked from seeing it."
Cradle: "Thank you for your information."

Cradle hangs up the phone from the tipster on a probable lead in the case to finding the murderer and bring him to justice. Next, Cradle calls the Duty Sergeant to put an APB (All Points Bulletin) to be on the lookout for a black 1993 Chevrolet Suburban truck with D.C. license plates but license plate number is unknown.

On July 6, the same day investigators released a wanted poster of a black truck. Washington, D.C. police chief Charles S. Wilson said, " investigators was searching for this vehicle throughout the D.C. Metropolitan Area".

Now, Cradle prepares to drive over to the White House to talk to both Secret Service Agents Robert Gates and Richard Spriggs. He flashed his MPD detective

o

badge to the roving Secret Service officer with his dog in tow alongside his Ford Crown Victoria. The Secret Service officer inside the guard post hits the switch opening up White House gate allowing Cradle to drive into the circular drive on the North Portico and parked his car there.

He briskly walks up the steps past the Marine Sergeant posted at the entrance way and proceeds on in, Cradle spots a Secret Service agent in the hallway and asks him, "Please call Agent Gates on your radio." Agent Gates shows up about five minutes after he was summoned on the radio.

Agent Gates shakes hands with Detective Michael Cradle and asks him, "What is the purpose of your visit here today"

Cradle, responds by saying, " I am here to speak about the murder of Richard Royster."

Gates, "Okay, no problem." He leads him down the hallway to an office they can talk in private.

"Have a seat Detective Cradle," Gates,, says. Cradle, ''Thank you Agent Gates" " I understand you was the last person to see Richard Royster alive prior to his murder." says Cradle

"Yes", Gates responds

Cradle, "When did you see Richard Royster?" "I saw him on his way out of the door on the afternoon of June 21, 1993"

Cradle, "How did he look" "He look happy and upbeat" says Gates.

Cradle, "Do you speak as he was leaving?" "Yes, I asked him how was he doing? "He said he was fine and smiled at me."

Gates Cradle, "Thank you to taking the time out of your busy schedule to talk to me." "Your are welcome Detective"

Gates responds Cradle, "Could you do me a big favor and call Agent Richard Spriggs to meet with me here."

Gates, "Sure Detective, anything I can do to help you with this case.'

o

Gates immediately called Agent Spriggs to come over and meet with Detective Cradle in the small White House office. Secret Service Agent Spriggs showed up 10 minutes after he was called. He had just finished having lunch in the White House cafeteria, a meal of a cheeseburger, fries and a coke.

Gates introduces Agent Spriggs to Detective Cradle. " I would like to introduce you to Detective Cradle"
 Gates says. Spriggs responds, "Please to meet you Detective." Cradle, " I was just here talking to your fellow agent Gates when I thought it would be a great idea to speak to you as well.
 Spriggs takes a seat and faces across from Cradle.
Cradle, " What time did you discover the body of Richard Royster"
 Spriggs, "It was 6:15 p.m, when I went the office of White House Counsel Richard Royster and witness him slumped over on his desk in a pool of blood."
 Cradle, "What did you do the next after you discovered his body."

Spriggs, "I placed the 911 call to the Metropolitan Police Department in which an operator answered and told me to don't touch anything and wait outside of the office until police arrived on the scene."
Cradle, "Thank Agent Spriggs."

Spriggs, " I stayed posted outside of Royster's office until the police arrived at approximately 7:06 p.m."

Cradle: "Would be so kind as provide with me with a copy of the White House surveillance tape from June 21, 1993 from 6:00-7:00 p,m,"
 Spriggs, "Sure I will be glad to provide you with the tape of that particular day and time Detective."
 Cradle, "Thank you Agent Spriggs, you have been very helpful to me." Spriggs, "You are welcome Detective Cradle."
 Cradle, Thanks again to you both Agents Gates and Spriggs.

o

Cradle walks out of the office, decides to go around to see Royster's office on the second floor of the West Wing of the White House, after a month had passed the murder had taken place.

Cradles walks into Royster's office in which had been cleaned out top to bottom of boxes, books, files and mementos of the man who occupied it. He searched it thoroughly for any remnant of evidence that may have been overlooked by the police, detectives and the FBI.

After fifteen minutes had gone by looking around Royster's office, Cradle decide to leave the premises of the White House and gets into his car and proceeds out of the opened White House gate back onto Pennsylvania Avenue.

The Washington Press Corps had already begun raising probing questions about Royster's death and how the White House was handling of it. The murder of Richard Royster at the White House is one of the biggest news worthy events of 1993!

White House inconsistencies in the handling the aftermath of Royster's death further fueled frenzy rumors of his misconduct.

The handling of the boxed up files in Royster's office set off an early feeding frenzy by the press with accusations of a cover-up and obstruction of justice of an outgoing investigation of his murder.
Yet it was not until certain members of the press--notably Lawrence Ross at the New York Post--began to hypothesize openly that Royster was murdered by pro Israeli terrorists and spies operating in the United States. Ross's reporting earned him the respect of the former FBI director fired by Reid, who wrote the Post reporter a letter detailing how Royster had been heavily involved with a power struggle between the Justice Department and the FBI. Because of this direct conflict the FBI was not allowed to investigate Royster's death.

Carnegie Andrew Miller's newspaper, the Pittsburgh Tribune-Review hired Lawrence Ross after he left the New York Post. The efforts to cast Royster's death

o

as more just a murder coincided with Miller's funding of the "Tennessee Project," a $2.8 million program funded at the conservative magazine The American Spectator to unearth damaging information on the Reid's according to the New York Times.

The billionaire also contributed large sums of money over the years to conservative media organizations like the Western Journalism Center, Accuracy in Media and the National Taxpayers Union, all of which drove home highly negative coverage in the Royster case.

As the story gathered speed and critical mass, papers such as the New York Times and the Washington Post began their own forays into the questions of why Royster was murdered. If nothing else, there was money to made by the media organizations spinning nefarious to kill Richard Royster even more.

A major fault in Ross and other investigations, though, are the lack of any plausible alternative scenario as to how Royster met his end.

The "profilers" almost all though the killer of Richard Royster was angry white man driving a black truck, acting alone,a clever and shrewd killer who knew the D.C. area so well he must live here. None of this, it seems, was true. The killer did not really know the area. He was not white. He did not own a black Chevrolet Suburban. Far from being a clever individual, he was dumb as a rock or a fence post. How did the media get it all wrong?

The profilers which was used on MSNBC consisted of ex-FBI Special Agents or police profilers or private investigators who had spent their entire careers working on similar cases.

Their conclusions were not only reasonable, they were identical to those of the profilers for the "task force." In these big task forces,there is going to be a lot of disagreement about what gets out and what gets released to the public. The reason being is there is a lot of egos involved in it.

o

Moreover, it was the task force, based on witness testimony, that out the one word out on the black Suburban truck and "box trucks" that mislead the media and caused police to maybe let a killer slip through their Dragnet and roadblocks.

Several announcements was repeatedly broadcasted on his police car radio: Twelve (12) black Chevrolet Suburban trucks has been stopped in and around the D.C. Metropolitan Area in the past several days.

The last black truck identified was reportedly stopped on Constitution Avenue between U.S. Botanical Gardens and the U.S. Capitol. A U.S. Capitol Hill Police Sergeant stopped the black Chevy Suburban driving along Constitution Avenue NW and searched the truck when the driver did not provide proof of insurance such as an insurance card. .

The search turned up what appeared to be a mobile sniper's nest, complete with a loaded .22 caliber rifle and scope, silencer, guns ports and wooden kitchen chairs mounted in the cargo area.

The driver told the Sergeant, he had purchased the truck for fifteen hundred dollars cash money ($1,500.00) on yesterday from a lady he met along with his partner at Starbucks in Arlington, Virginia.

Both him and and his partner did not take the time to simply look into the back of truck, prior to picking up the vehicle from the lady's garage. This seemed like an interesting story to tell police when any reasonable person would check out both the interior and exterior of a vehicle before purchase whether or not it was used or new.

The driver and his partner was arrested by the U.S. Capitol Hill Police and the black Suburban truck was impounded. D.C. Metropolitan Police Department picked two men up and took them for lock-up at the Sixth Distinct Precinct after U.S. Capitol Hill Police called them for transport.

o

These two men are unrelated to the search for the killer and will be arraigned and sentenced for the possession of a firearm and driving an uninsured vehicle.

The saga of the search for the black Chevrolet Suburban was over now since none of them was the one that took the killer of Richard Royster away not to be seen again in the city of Washington, DC and the surrounding areas of Maryland and Virginia which is regularly referred to as the DMV. People who live outside of the DMV think us locals are talking about the Department of Motor Vehicle.

It seems like one black Chevrolet Suburban would be easy to find but No, it is like a needle in a haystack. Cradle has hit these brickwalls before in his illustrious career as D.C. Homicide Detective. He knows how to best deal with the situation by driving across town to see some promising young people.

He retreated over to the Boys & Girls Club on Capitol Hill to check in on his mentees there. Working with young people is Cradle's way of dealing with and managing the pressure and stress of his job in a professional and dignified manner. This time he was not giving an usual lecture to them on staying in school and making good grades but to share with them his love of writing movies scripts and making movies. Cradle's face lights up when he talks about his passion of writing, directing and producing movies like a proud parent, whose wife just had a baby. The children feels like they have met a real movie star in Cradle but he tells them, " I am a lousy actor but a better director and producer of film." The kids burst out in laughter when Cradle shares this fact with them.

On July 7, Cradle arrives back into his office where he receives the White House surveillance video tape. He opens the official White House milan legal size envelope containing a handwritten note from Secret Service Richard Spriggs on Secret Service stationery which reads:

July 6, 1993

o

Detective Cradle:

As per your request on July 6 for a copy of the White House surveillance video tape from Friday, June 21, 1993.

Enclosed is a tape for "your eyes only."

Sincerely,

Agent Spriggs
U.S. Secret Service

P.S. If you need anything else, please feel free to call me (202) 456-7000

Cradle places the tape in his video recorder and player connected to the television in his office, turns off the light and begins viewing the tape. First, he sees White House staff going about their merry way in the hallways, butlers and maids on duty, Secret Service agents patrolling the perimeter, Marines on their posts and the President and First Lady walking hand in hand together. Nothing could be found strange or out of place on the tape. So he had to fast forward the tape to the time frame that the murder of Richard Royster took place.

The video reveals a man dressed in a Secret Service uniform walking into the door of the White House past another Service Service and proceeds down the long hallway towards the West Wing, swiftly passes the Oval Office to the office up the steps to the second floor to the office suite occupied by Richard Royster. Before entering the office, the killer slips on a black mask to cover his face from sight and pair of black leather gloves so no fingerprints could be found on the door knob.

Now the killer proceeds into Royster's office shoot him at 6:00p.m in which the clock on the tape reflects and rushes out of the office and runs down the long hallway, removing ski mask and gloves and places his gun back into it holster along the way. Immediately he gets to the front door where two Marines are posted and escapes out of the door. The killer is on the run. Cradle stops the video tape at this point. He walks out of his office and down the hall to a vacant office, enters the office which is pitch black and does not bother to turn on the light. He wants to be

o

in complete darkness to think, reflect and visualize in his mind what he saw on the video.

He stays in the dark, vacant office for thirty minutes and walks out and back to his office. He decides to take the video tape to the forensic crime downstairs for evaluation by the forensic specialist. forensic specialist pops the video in his , video player. Cradle instructs him to go to the segment of the tape when the killer the premises of the White House, shoots Royster and exits out of the door of the White House.

It has been persistently reported that the video tapes that would have recorded Richard Royster leaving the White House and his return on the day of his death have vanished from the secure vault they are normally stored in. Also, a surveillance camera records whoever enters and leaves this vault as well. The video tapes that would have recorded who took the tapes from the vault have also reportedly vanished. The White House and the FBI have never denied this. If the story is false, it could be finally laid to rest by simply producing the video surveillance tapes in question. Why have the FBI and the White House failed to do so?

Now, Cradle tells him to slow down the tape to hopefully made out the face of the killer, forensic specialist scrolls into the tape to discover a blurry pale white of a man with Hispanic features. Now, Cradle has something to go on and work with so to speak, a likeness of the killer. He tells the forensic specialist to stop the tape and return it. Next, he goes down to the third floor where a police artist is located.

He gives the police artist the physical description of the man shown on the tape: 5'9 175 lbs, dark-skinned " Hispanic looking man" to interpret the data into the criminal identification system. After fishing through hundreds, thousands and possibly hundred thousands of criminals in the NCIC system, a picture comes up of man with dark skin, long and black hair, ,with Hispanic features along with a mustache and goatee. Cradle would later describe the man to a sketch artist for the Washington Post. The sketch was published in the Washington Post as well as the Washington Times newspapers.

o

Also, the D.C. Metropolitan Police Department created a flyer, which was printed up in up several hundreds of his pictures to passed out by patrol officers throughout the city of Washington. Also, these officers posted a copies of the flyers on street lamp posts, community centers, Metro buses and trains as well.

The next day which was July 8 , detectives and patrol officers began receiving the flyers with the killer's picture on it. The object of this manhunt is the man who picture is displayed on the flyer they now are displaying to the general public.

The Washington-Arlington-Alexandria-DC-VA-MD-WV Metropolitan Statistical Area. becomes the target search area , wider and larger than life. The real result is the local communities being on the cutting edge across scores of miles.

Cradle was riding along in his car on the southwest waterfront which is called "The Wharf" when he received a call patched through by police dispatcher at Metropolitan Police Department from anonymous caller who saw the telephone number posted on a flyer in a tree in Vienna, Virginia.

Caller: " I was out walking my Doberman Pinscher near the Wolf Trap Filene Center when I discovered a black duffle lying near a couple of trees, I open the bag and found a badly soiled Secret Service all uniform balled up and stuffed in the bag.

Cradle: "Where do you live?"
Caller: "I live on 419 Mill Street SE Vienna, Virginia."
Cradle: " I will be right over to pick up that duffle bag."

Cradle immediately hangs up his cell phone. Then, He makes an U turn to head west from southwest to Constitution Avenue onto the exit to I- 66. Traffic is always heavy heading to the Northern Virginia area but it is after rush hour and it is moving smooth and steady for the next fifteen minutes when it slows due to road

o

construction on the shoulder of the road, Now it is moving again smooth for twenty minutes where Cradle takes the exit for 123 Vienna, he drives past the Metro Station and makes a right turn on Main Street and drive the next 5 minutes until he gets to Mill Street where he makes a right turn. Cradle drives the street about ½ block until he spots the house number 419, he parks his car and walks up to the house and rings the doorbell, the gentleman opens the door as Cradle proceeds to flashes his badge to him.

"I am Detective Michael Cradle , I spoke to you by phone a few hours ago."
"Good afternoon, Detective Cradle, I am Daniel Rush, I spoke to you on the phone this morning about finding the black duffle bag."
Cradle: "Nice to meet you Mr. Rush."
Rush: "Wait a minute, so I can go get the duffle back for you."
Cradle: "Okay Mr. Rush."
Rush" Here is the black duffle bag Detective Cradle" as he hands over to him.

Cradle, says "Thank you Mr. Rush, Have a nice day" Mr. Rush shuts his door to his home. Cradle gets back into his car drives back down Mill Street and makes a left onto Main Street to head back on I-66 east to Washington. The traffic is moving swift and smooth as he head east on I-66 on his way back to D.C.

Once Cradle arrives back at MPD headquarters about thirty minutes, he turns over the duffle bag to the crew in the forensic lab for evaluation. He hope that some fingerprints will be found on the bag as well as on the clothing of the killer. The forensic lab crew began immediately working on the duffle bag. They performed extensive analyses of the physical evidence of the duffle bag found by Mr. Rush, the man who lives in Vienna, VA, that found it Wolf Trap Filene Center.

The Wolf Trap Filene Center located at America's National Park for the Performing Arts, Wolf Trap's majestic Filene Center provides the Washington, DC metropolitan area with a magical outdoor venue for world class performances of every genre. Operated in partnership with the National Park Service, the Filene Center houses over ninety (90) performances annually from late May to early September..

o

Among the tests conducted by the forensic lab: an examination of the bag for fingerprints of the killer; a chemical and physical comparison of gunpowder and lead residue on Royster's clothing with that of the killer's discarded Secret Service uniform; an analysis of hair fiber and lint found on the uniform and a fingerprint analysis. The forensic lab has completed their work on the duffle in which the forensic scientist could create his report of his findings to be left on Cradle's desk on the next morning.

On July 9, Cradle walks into his office to find the forensic lab report on the black duffle bag on his desk. Four experts in the field of forensic pathology reviewed and analyzed the evidence which was the duffle bag submitted by Detective Cradle. Cradle began to read the forensic lab report:

The black duffle bag was examined for fingerprints but none was found. The conclusion is the killer wore physical examination gloves carrying and handling the bag.

The Secret Service uniform is the "real McCoy", the genuine item worn by the United States Secret Service Uniformed Division consisted of white shirt complete with Secret Service insignia and U.S. flag patch along with black slacks with a gold stripe running along both legs of the pants.

No other items were found in the black duffle bag by the forensic lab team. The bag did not even contain a name tag identifying the owner of it. How strange is that?

About half of the day is almost over when Cradle received anonymous tip from a caller at his desk, The caller relays to Cradle that he discover in a luggage storage locker number 402 located at Dulles International Airport a Secret Service officer hat and badge. Cradle says "Thank you to the caller."

He hangs up, he walks out of his office, to take elevator downstairs to head out the rear of the building to pick up his car. He drives the street makes a left on fifth street and drives down to the intersection where Pennsylvania Avenue and

o

Constitution Avenues meet And proceeds down Constitution Avenue onto the ramp near State Department to I-66. He runs into some early rush traffic at 2:30 p.m. but no bottlenecks to slow him down.

Washington Dulles International Airport(ISATA: IAD, ICAO: KIAD) is a public airport located 25 miles (40 km) west of the central business district of Washington, D.C.in Dulles, Virginia. It is located partly in Chantilly and partly in Dulles, west of Herndon and southwest of Sterling. In 1958, the village of Willard was torn down to make room for Dulles,and countless roads, homes, stores and schools were demolished to make room for runaways, concourses and other features. It serves the greater Washington, D.C. metropolitan area.

He arrives at Dulles at 3:05 p.m.,He enters the main terminal area, before he goes to the locker he puts on a pair of examination gloves. Next, he proceeds to the luggage storage locker and goes to locker number 402 and open it and discovers the Secret Service hat and badge intact in the locker. He pulls out a large evidence bag to place the Secret Service hat and badge into it. He walks back out of the main terminal of Dulles to his car parked out with the placard in it "On Official MPD Police Business" Cradle glances at his watch 3:30 p.m. rush hours is not full and effect on both Beltway. He is back in his car with the large evidence bag on the seat driving along I-66 proceeding east, the traffic is moving not stop and go like most days. Cradle is happy about that he can get back to headquarters at least before 5:00 p.m.

He has driven back into Arlington passing by the large white building overlooking the highway, CACI Headquarters. CACI provides information solutions and services in support of national security missions and government transformation for intelligence, defense, and federal civilian customers. CACI is Fortune's magazine's World's Admired Company in the Information Technology (IT) Services industry. In view of light traffic , he is back downtown where MPD police headquarters is located. He parks his car outside in the reserved spaces in the rear of the building, He get out of his car carrying the large evidence bag containing

o

the Secret Service hat and badge. He drops off the evidence bag with the forensic lab for evaluation.

He takes the elevator back up to his office on the fifth floor. He prepares to wrap up for the day since it is now 4:30 p.m, Cradle is dead tired and plans to go straight home as the clock strikes 5:00 p.m. It had been a quite a productive day and now it was time to unwind from it all. The forensic lab got busy at work on examining the Secret Service hat and badge as Cradle departed for home as his shift ended for the day. The forensic lab will have their report of their findings ready for him on his desk tomorrow morning.

On July 10, Cradle is feeling re- energize, ready to get back to work on the case, as he takes a seat in his chair, back at his desk Then, he notices the forensic lab report lying in front of him on his desk.

Immediately, he begins to read it. The forensic scientist states the Secret Service hat has a name tag in it belong to Agent Bryce. The badge is a standard issued badge used by the Secret Service for their sworn officers. Cradle deduces from this he is "being played like a puppet on a string within the government bureaucracy." All roads and sources are leads it way back

Cradle places a call to Service Service Agent Spriggs.

Cradle: "Hello Spriggs, This is Cradle"
Spriggs: "Cradle ,what can I do for you?
Cradle: "Can you provide me with copy of your logs from June 21, the day Royster was murdered?"
Spriggs: "Detective, I will be happy to provide you with the logs."
Cradle: "Spriggs, I will be over to the White House in about fifteen minutes."
Spriggs: "Cradle, I will see you soon along with the logs."
Cradle: "Thanks"

Cradle hangs up the phone and rushes out of his office carrying the Secret Service hat and badge, proceeds to catch the elevator downstairs, out of the backdoor of

o

police headquarters to his parked car. He gets into his car, driving down the street making a left turn on fifth street, next making a right turn on Pennsylvania Avenue passing by National Archives, Navy Memorial, Robert F. Kennedy Department of Justice Building, J. Edgar Hoover FBI Building, The Old Post Office, John Wilson District Building. Then a sharp right turn by the Treasury Building and left back onto Pennsylvania Avenue to the White House North Portico gate manned by Secret Service Uniformed Division guard. Cradle lower his car window to flash his MPD Detective badge at the guard. who flags his car onto the White House driveway in which he parks his car in the circle. Cradle gets out of his car, carrying the Secret Service hat and badge. He walks up the short steps passed two U.S. Marines posted at the door. Cradle shows his badge to the Marines on post as they open the door for him to enter the premises of the White House. Standing inside near the door is Secret Service Agent Spriggs as Detective Cradle walks in, carrying the Secret Service hat and badge.

Spriggs reached out to shake Cradle hand. Cradle says, "The reason that I am here is to return Secret Service agent Bryce's hat and badge." Spriggs: "Where did you find these items at." Cradle: " I picked them up at Dulles Airport in a luggage locker after I was tipped off about them being there." Spriggs: "Great."
Cradle: "Will you radio Agent Bryce about his hat and badge" Spriggs: "Sure, I will call him right now." Cradle: "Thank you Spriggs." Agent Bryce enter the long corridor in ten minutes after being called by Spriggs. Spriggs introduces Detective Cradle. Spriggs says, "This is Homicide Detective Cradle from D.C. Metropolitan Police." Bryce; "Nice to meet you Detective Cradle." Cradle reaches out to shake Agent Bryce's hand. Cradle, "Here is your hat and badge that was found out at Dulles Airport in a luggage locker." Bryce, " I did not realize my hat and badge had stolen from my locker here at the White House."
Cradle: " I think the killer of Richard Royster stole your hat and badge since he was wearing a Secret Service uniform to commit the murder." Bryce: "Thanks Detective Cradle for returning my hat and badge to me." Cradle: "You are welcome Agent Bryce." Bryce takes his hat and badge and walks away.
Cradle says to Agent Spriggs, "What about the Secret Service logs you promised me." Agent Spriggs, "Detective Cradle here is the logs you requested." Spriggs

o

hands over a copy of the logs to Cradle. Cradle reaches to grab the Secret Service folder containing the logs from Spriggs. Cradle says "Thank you Agent Spriggs." Spriggs, "You are welcome Detective," Now, Cradle walks out of the door of the White House as Agent Spriggs waves good bye to him, he proceeds to drive out of the White House gate on his way back to MPD headquarters. In about five (5) minutes with light traffic, Cradle has parked his car and catches the elevator to his fifth office. He anxiously to begin reading the Secret Service logs.

According to the Secret Service logs, at 7:00 p,m,, the day of Royster's death, an entry alarm went off in Royster;s office. This has never been explained or even referred to in an official reports on Royster's death. According to Secret Service logs, at 7:10 p.m. that evening, a group listed as "MIG" logged into the White House. Aide Rhonda Bethune arrived at the same time. April Evans-Williams believes MIG stands for Maintenance and Installation Group, a group of experts who handle such things as sales and surveillance equipment. MIG and Rhonda Bethune left together.

According to Secret Service logs, at about 7:15 p.m. Washington time, White House aide Helen Woods called the governor's mansion in Nashville, Tennessee, to tell the governor Royster had been murdered at the White House in his office. The call was received by trooper Perry Edge. Hed states that Ms. Woods was crying. Edge saye he promptly called several people to tell them the news. Among them was trooper Nick Peterson and former Tennessee state police commander Lawrence Reynolds. Both men have signed affidavits attesting to these calls. The time estimates vary, but all three men agree the calls took place during rush-hour traffic in Nashville.

No official explanation has been given to a to account for these comings and goings. Rhonda Bethune was one of the White House aide who reportedly searched Richard Royster's office.

Did MIG assist her by opening Royster's safe in his White House office?

Did MIG disable the entry alarm system?

o

Eva von Trappe (ET) was a member of George Hoover Wilson Brad's Staff during his presidency. She served as a computer surveillance expert. She worked with a team that has been described as Brad's "plumbers unit." In this capacity, she often worked with David Getz(DG), an FBI agent. According to von Trappe, Getz sounded drunk and extremely excited when he called her northern California home from Washington, D.C., at 11:00 p.m., June 21, 1993 (the day of Royster's death). She says she records all phone conversations. This is a partial transcript of her alleged exchange with Getz:

DG: "We did him! We did him!"
ET: "Did who"?"
DG: "Richard Royster."
ET: "What do you mean?"
DG: "We did him!"
ET: "Well, where did you do him?"
DG: "Well, we did him in his office on the second floor of the West Wing."
ET: "Okay, I guess his office is a good place to do him as any other place."
DG: " Better than dumping him off in a queer park to send Reid and his queer wife a message."
ET: "Absolutely!"

Cradle finishes his reading exercise of the Secret Service logs. The chronology of the activities was noteworthy. There are now good reasons to doubt the White House's claim it did not learn of Royster's death until 8: 30 p.m.

The Washington Times filed a Freedom of Information Act request for copies of the White House logs for that particular evening. This FOIA request was vehemently denied without explanation. Also, the relevant phone logs at the governor's mansion in Nashville have vanished.

As the Washington Post put it in a July 10, 1993, new article, "After originally describing Royster's death as a shock that mystified the White House and President Reid, the White House over the past several days and weeks--in the light and face of revelations from friends and law enforcement officials--acknowledged a far more depressed and unhappy officials than it first described.

The week ends on a high note for Cradle with the discovery of Secret Service uniform, hat and badge as well as capping it off the reading of Secret Service phone logs.

The distribution of the flyers bearing the likeness of the killer began paying dividends over the weekend with the "Terry stop" of five (5) dark skinned Hispanic looking men by Metropolitan Police patrol officers. In the United States, a " Terry stop" is a brief detention of a person by police on a reasonable suspicion of involvement in criminal activity but short of probable cause to arrest. The name derives from **Terry v. Ohio**, 392 U.S. 1 (1968), in which the **Supreme Court of the United States** held that police may briefly detain a person whom they reasonably suspect is involved in criminal activity. Each detained motorist stopped was requested to report in on Monday at or around 12 noon for a police lineup, since each one bears a striking resemblance to the killer of Richard Royster.

The goal of any investigation is to find the truth. Truth is the goal in every criminal investigation. In order to prove it, many types of evidence are used, including eyewitnesses. We have all experienced a time in our life when a person knows something we do not, and as hard as they might to remain neutral, their face often limits at the answer. During criminal investigations we must guard against this tell. Through the use of a double blind lineup, we are one step closer to uncovering the truth. The benefit of a double blind lineup is that it only keeps investigators for them to do so, and thus keeps the process fair.

"Six-pack" is slang for a single sheet of paper with a photo of the suspect and five others who bear a resemblance. The "six pack" is one method that has long been having a role in how law enforcement officers identify suspects recently been called into question; with other alternatives being explored for improved accuracy.

On the morning of July 13, Cradle arrived back in his office at 9 p.m. to handwritten note by the Chief that a phone lineup will take place at 12 noon.

o

A police lineup is where an eyewitness identifies a suspect out of a group of five or six other people who fits the suspect description. The eyewitness will be instructed to stand behind a one-way mirror and point out the person that they believed committed the crime. Police lineup are derived from English criminal law and procedure.

According to Devlin (1976) lineups were instituted through a Middlesex magistrate's order in mid 19th century. They were intended as a 'fair" replacement for the practices of courtroom identification, and showups, which was widely used in 19th century England, but widely recognized as potentially unfair to the defendant. Their origin indicates that the notion of "fairness" is their raison d'etre. They are intended to secure an identification that can potentially incriminate someone, but also is fair to those who are subjected to, particularly those who are innocent of the crime. There is some research into using other methods of photo-lineup that involves the witness sequentially viewing photographs rather than simultaneously. The sequential method is considered more accurate because it prevents the witness from looking at all the suspects and merely selecting the person that most resembles the guilty person. In the United Kingdom (UK) police forces use Video Identification Parade Electronic Recording (VIPER), a digital system wherein witnesses view video recording of suspects and unrelated volunteers. UK which prides itself on it eyewitness identification procedures.

Eyewitness identification is one of the most potent and effective tools available to police and prosecutors. It is compelling and time after time, it convinces juries of the guilt of a defendant. The real problem is sometimes eyewitness identifications are WRONG at least fifty percent (50%) of the time!

At around 11:30 a.m. first of the men arrived at D.C. Metropolitan Police Department headquarters downtown. Also, the anonymous caller who offered Cradle his first tip of he saw man running through Lafayette Parking wearing a Secret Service uniform arrives as a witness for the police lineup, passing through the metal detector, Cradle directs him to the elevator in which they ride together to

o

the lower level in a room where the lineup will take place. Next, other four men arrive respectfully at 11:35, 11:40, 11:45 and 11:50 a.m. Cradle has all of the five (5) men to assemble together in a room adjacent to the room where the lineup will take place. He gives them each a number with a string attached to it, each man places the sign bearing the number, over his head and around his neck with the numbers 1,2,3,4 and 5. It is now 12 noon, the five men of similar height, build, and complexion stand side-by-side, both facing, bearing their numbers and in profile in the room. Also, the room contains markings on the wall to aid identifying the man's height.

The anonymous tip caller called arrives for the police lineup, he introduces himself to Cradle as Thomas Kirby. He is 34, 5'9", 165lbs, Caucasian man.

Cradle, responds"Nice to meet you Mr. Kirby."
Thomas Kirby, A pleasure to meet you Detective Cradle."

Mr. Kirby enters the room behind the one-way mirror to allow him as the witness to remain anonymous even to them. Cradle shows Kirby the police flyer bearing the likeness of a dark skinned Hispanic looking man as the possible suspect.

Cradle: " Please look at the flyer closely to see that any of the men resemble the man in the flyer."

Kirby looks at the flyer closely to compare it to the men in the police lineup. He analyzes and compares the flyer with the men assembled in the lineup .

Kirby: "None of the men bear any likeness to the man in the flyer."
Cradle: " Now, Mr. Kirby looks closely and carefully at the men in the lineup."
Kirby: "Detective Cradle, no man present looks like the one in your flyer."
Cradle: "Thank you Mr. Kirby for your assistance, You are free to leave."
Kirby: "You are welcome Detective Cradle."
Mr. Kirby caller leaves the room and catches the next available elevator back upstairs and exits the building.

o

Next, Cradle enters the room behind the one way mirror where the men are lined up. He tells them to take their numbers off. Also, he tells them they are dismissed and now free to go home. He personally thanks them and shakes each one of their hands as the individuals leave the police lineup room in the subbasement of the D.C. Metropolitan Police Department. All the men enter the elevator together and ride it back upstairs to exit the building and go their separate ways.

It is 1:30 p.m. in the afternoon, Cradle decide to have lunch since the police lineup is over and completed. He walks out of the door of police headquarters heading west down the street and cross over to the other side of the street to where the Subway sandwich shop is located. He walks in and places his order for a 6" inch turkey breast sub sandwich with lettuce, tomatoes, green pepper, sweet peppers, hot relish light mayo, and mustard along with a medium coke and lays potato chips. Cradle takes a seat near the window overlooking D.C. Superior Court building across the street. He takes a bite out of his sandwich, thinking to himself how the events of his investigation is being played out in the past several weeks since Richard Royster was murdered at the White House. His job is nonstop and never ending since no murder resulted from the police lineup he held today. He finishes his lunch at 2:30 p.m. and walks back down the street into police headquarters, taking the elevator back up to his office on the fifth floor. He takes a seat down at his desk, starts opening and reading his mail for the day. No new developments of interest in the case. He decides to knock off work earlier and go for a jog around the Tidal Basin near the Jefferson Memorial. It is a hot July afternoon in the Nation's Capitol but the humidity levels is low for a chance allowing Cradle to get into a good jog.

Instead of seeing a proper homicide investigation, we have seen Royster's death become mired in a morass of lies, confusion, and conflicting evidence. Faced with this labyrinth, there is not any hope of putting together a challenge-proof of over 100 items is unrealistic. Nonetheless, Cradle is confident ninety percent (90%) of these assertions will hold up with time. For any reasonable, rational person, the weight of ninety (90)- plus discrepancies must still remain staggering.

o

When the kitchen gets too hot, we have to douse the flames of public indignation with few repercussions as possible. In a lot of murder cases, as the room grows too much hot to handle for some people, they have to step down and resign from their high level positions. "Two hot to handle, Too cold to hold" is the lyrics from a probably rap song from Bobby Brown in the movie "Ghostbusters" would be applicable to this situation.

CHAPTER FOUR
EXODUS

"The men the American people admire most extravagantly are the greatest liars; the men they detest most violently are those who try to tell them the truth."
H.L. Mencken

The primary focus had been on Detective Michael Cradle's investigation into the murder homicide of Richard Royster for the past several weeks but now it's was time to take a glimpse into the agency with the arduous task of protecting the President and First Family.

The developments come with the U.S. Secret Service, which protects the president and his family, in the midst of a shake-up after a series of scandals and security breaches at the White House. A US lawmaker leading a congressional inquiry into the secret service raised questions on Tuesday, June 14 about a White House volunteer possible involvement in a prostitution scandal that rocked the agency three years ago.

The U.S. Secret Service investigates thousands of incidents a year of individuals threatening the President of the United States.

The Director of the Secret Service is appointed by the President of the United States.

The Secret Service's initial responsibility was to investigate counterfeiting of U.S. currency, which was rampant during the Civil War. The agency involved into the United States first domestic intelligence and counterintelligence agency.
Many of the agency's mission were later taken over by subsequent agencies such as Federal Bureau of Investigations, Alcohol, Tobacco and Firearms, and Internal Revenue Service.

The Secret Service was the first U.S. domestic intelligence and counterintelligence agency. Domestic intelligence collection and counterintelligence were vested in the Federal Bureau of Investigation (FBI) upon the FBI's creation in 1908.

As of 1993, the U.S. Secret Service has over 3,500 employees, 1.600 Special Agents, 650 Uniformed Division Officers, and 1,000 technical and administrative employees. Also, the Secret Service has agents assigned to 86 field offices and

o

headquarters in Washington, D.C. with an annual budget of $550,000,000,000 million dollars.

Special agents serve on protective detail, special teams or sometime investigate certain financial and homeland security-related crimes.

Representative Joseph Carney, chairman of the House oversight and government reform subcommittee on national security, said in an interview that the White House had new questions to answer in light of information he has received from secret service whistleblowers as well as a report in Tuesday's Washington Post. White House officials were adamant in denying involvement by anyone on their team in the incident. The scandal led to the firing of more than half-dozen secret service agents who had hired prostitutes while on assignment in Bogota with President Burd for the 1990 summit.

After the incident was publicized, the Secret Service implemented new rules for its personnel. The rules prohibit personnel from visiting "non-reputable establishments and from consuming alcohol less than ten (10) hours before starting work. Additionally, they restrict who is allowed in hotel rooms.

A few weeks later, stories emerged of Secret Service hiring strippers and prostitutes prior to Reid's 1993 visit to the Dominican Republic.

Carney, a Republican, suggested that based on his conversations with the whistleblowers, he feels that the White House might be covering up some information.

The White House disputed claims that there was any attempt to suppress information related to a young volunteer on the White House advance team and whether he too, had a prostitute in his hotel room.

"As was reported more than three years ago, the White House conducted an internal review that did not identify any appropriate behavior on the part of the White House advance team." White House spokesman John Campbell said. " And of course there was no White House interference with an inspector general investigation."

The Washington Post reviewed records from the Bogota hotel where the advance team stayed that identified the prostitute and appeared to show she had signed in to visit the room with the White House volunteer, identified by the newspaper as Rickey Dees.

Rickey Dees is the son of a major Democratic donor, is now employed by the State Department. Michael Richards, a Washington lawyer representing Rickey Dees, said allegations that Dees brought a prostitute to his room during the 1990 trip to Bogota "don't ring true."

In September 1990, the Department of Justice's internal watchdog wrote in a summary of his investigation that there was a hotel record suggesting a member of Burd's team might have been involved in the Bogota prostitution scandal. That summary report was sent to Congress.

Edward T. Charles, the acting inspector general at the time, said in a summary that the employee, described by the administration as a volunteer, "may have had contact with foreign national" and may have been affiliated with the White House advance operation, "according to a letter to lawmakers obtained at the time by the Associated Press.

Charles cited a hotel registry obtained by his investigators as documentary evidence.

Also at the time, the White House said its own review concluded that a guest, possibly a prostitute signed in at the hotel front desk to visit the room assigned to the White House worker, but the hotel logbook was deemed false and there was no other evidence to corroborate the allegation.

o

But the Post reported on Tuesday that the lead investigator on the case later told Senate aides that he felt pressured by his supervisor to withhold evidence and that political decisions were made in an election year.

Carney said he had learned, as reported in the published account, that staffers who raised questions about the White House role were put on administrative leave.

"All signs point to a major cover-up but I want to give the White House a chance to explain itself," Carney said. He said the White House has not precisely how and why it was able to clear Dees of any wrongdoing. He said he planned to hold hearings on the matter.

The June 7 incident involving a Texas Army veteran who jumped the White House and was able to make it deep into the Executive Mansion before being stopped is now just one of the several embarrassing disclosures about lapses in presidential security involving the U.S. Secret Service.

Despite more than three hours of questioning by House lawmakers, Stephanie Henderson, the first female director of the secret service neglected to the murder of Richard Royster in the White House. Her failure to do so prompted Rep. Joseph Carney, R-South Dakota, to call for Henderson's resignation--or firing--in an exclusive interview with Fox News Tuesday night.

At Tuesday's hearing, Henderson said she was the one who briefs Reid on threats to his personal security and said she had briefed him only once this, for the June 21 Royster's murder." She also disclosed that shortly before the alleged Lou Hernandez, Texas Army veteran scaled the White House fence at least two of her uniformed officers recognized him from an earlier troubling encounter but did not approach him or report his presence to superiors.

Lawmakers were aghast, too, about a four-day delay in 1991 before the Secret Service realized a man had a fired a high-powered rifle at the White House, as reported by the Washington Post on the Sunday edition.

o

Henderson told the hearing security plan for protecting the White House for protecting the White House was not "properly executed" on June 21. The Secret Security's story about the extent of that breach changed late Monday after the Washington Post first reported that Hernandez got well past the front door of the White House. Previously it said Hernandez had been stopped just inside the front door. After several hours of questioning Tuesday, it remained unclear what and when Henderson knew about the incident.

The June 21 murder and security breaches was the latest black eyes for the failing agency. Henderson was named director of the U.S. Secret Service in March 1992, tapped by Burd to change the culture of an agency that was then marred by the Bogota prostitution scandal.

Several male U.S. Secret Service agents in an advance contingent before a presidential trip to Bogota, Columbia. had taken prostitutes back to their hotel rooms, according to investigations after the trip. A morning after the dispute between one agent and a woman over payment for her services led to the exposure of what happened and the ensuing investigations. Nine agents eventually resign or lost their jobs.

Who is Stephanie Henderson?

Henderson started her career in law enforcement as a young police officer in Orlando, Florida. She joined the U.S. Secret Service in 1983, working primarily in the Miami and Orlando field offices. Henderson became the Secret Service's chief of staff in 1990. Before that, she served on the protective details of Presidents George Hoover Wilson Burd and Thomas Jefferson Reid. She had been the assistant director of the agency's Office of Human Resources and Training, and held the title of deputy assistant director in the office of Protective Operations and the Office of Administration.

Calls for Henderson to leave her post grew after her poor performance during her testimony Tuesday on Capitol Hill and another bombshell revelation the same day that an armed security contractor was allowed to get into an elevator with the

o

President during a recent trip to the Centers for Disease Control in Atlanta, Georgia. Secret Service director testimony omits the elevator accident with President.

And New York's Charles Taney, the third-ranking Democrat in the U.S. Senate, had announced he would call for Henderson's resignation on Wednesday as well, though that was later canceled.

Republicans also had called for Henderson to step down as well.

"It's clear to me that the only way to solve the problem the Secret Service has is with new leadership, " Sen Graham Rudd of South Carolina said, "What Stephanie Henderson describes as mistakes are major security failures on multiple fonts."

Rudd said, "light security around President Reid is the worst possible signal to send to terrorists and our enemies around the world."

On Wednesday, July 15 Stephanie Henderson, the first female director of the U.S. Secret Service resigned in the aftermath of the Hernandez incident and subsequent congressional inquiry uncovering other security lapses including the murder of White House Counsel Richard Royster on June 21.

Attorney General Jaime Woods announced the resignation in an official Department of Justice statement. Woods said: "Today Stephanie Henderson, the Director of the United States Secret Service, offered her resignation, and I accepted it. I salute her thirty (30) years of distinguished service to the Secret Service and the Nation."

A source familiar with the situation told Fox News that Woods told Henderson the resignation would be effective immediately, after she offered it.

He also that the Department of Justice would take over an internal inquiry of the Secret Service and he would appoint of a new panel to review security standard operational procedures at the White House complex.

o

Joseph Duffy, formerly a special agent in charge of the Presidential Protective Division of the Secret Service, was named as interim director of the United States Secret Service Woods said in her statement.

After news of her resignation broke, lawmakers praised her decision to step down.

"The agency tasked with protecting the highest office in our land should be the crown jewel of federal law enforcement." Rep. Joseph Carney, who sits on the Oversight Committee, said in a statement Wednesday afternoon. "I will work with my colleagues and the Reid Administration towards returning the agency to the standards the President deserves."

Even some high-ranking Democrats had turned against Henderson, who was in the job for less than two years. In an interview on Wednesday, Rep William Woodrow, the top Democrat on the House Oversight Committee, where Tuesday's hearing took place, said he thought Henderson who he referred to as "this lady" -- "has to go."

The Maryland congressman reiterated this stance in an interview with CNN's Wolf Blitzer. "I want her to go if she cannot restore trust in the agency and if she cannot get the culture back in order," he said. The top Democrat on the committee who grilled Henderson, notably told National Public Radio (NPR) she is "not the best person to lead the agency"--though he later clarified he thinks she should go if she can't restore public trust.

But a Secret Service source told CNN there is an elaborate closed circuit video system, and that video is being dissected to establish new security protocols.

When Hernandez burst through the White House door, he pushed a female officer to the side. But the source said, "Gender was not a factor, she got one door secured but was pushed over while trying to get the second door shut."

An alarm box had been turned down near the front door at the White House after complaints by the White House usher's office that it was too loud.

o

A canine unit was not released to chase Hernandez, said the source because there were "too many friendlies around."

U.S. Secret Service vague with details to federal court following the fence jumping arrest.

News of Henderson's resignation came as new information is made available about the fence jumper came to light.

Lou Hernandez, 40 was indicted on Tuesday and pleaded not guilty on Wednesday before Magistrate Judge Judy M. Ross in U.S. District Court. Judge Ross ordered additional mental testing on the forty (40) year old Vietnam war veteran to determine whether he is competent to stand trial for the incident.

The White House fence jumper made it into the East Room of the White House.

Meanwhile, the inquiry continues into how the Army veteran launched over the White House fence and was able to sprint up to the front door, burst into the White House, darted past several layers of security, and run briskly into the ornate East Room before being apprehended.

Woods made sure to praise the overall work ethic of the Secret Service when she announced Henderson's resignation.

"It is worth repeating that the Secret Service is one of the finest official protection services in the world, consisting of men and women who are highly trained and skilled professionals prepared to put their own lives on the line in a second's notice for the people they protect ."

Henderson's departure, though, marked a sharp turnaround from a day earlier, when despite her rocky performance during the congressional testimony, the White House voiced support for her leadership. Asked Tuesday whether President Reid had confidence in the Secret Service Director, source said "absolutely."

Among those reports was the stark revelation that on June 1, a security contractor armed with a gun who had previously been arrested for assault rode on an elevator with President Reid and his security detail at the Centers for Disease Control and Prevention in Atlanta violating Secret Service protocol. The President was briefed on about the incident on Tuesday.

New and alarming details also emerged--seemingly by the day--about the multiple security failures in the June 1 intrusion. Not until late Monday was it reported that he made it into the East Room, a detail that was confirmed by Henderson during her testimony on Capitol Hill before the congressional committee.

Woods said that she now agrees that a "panel of independent experts" should review the June 1 incident--something that had been called for by lawmakers. She said a panel will submit its assessment and recommendations by November 15.

" I will also request that the panel advise me about whether it believes, given the series of events, there should be a review of broader issues concerning the U.S. Secret Service. The security of the White House complex should be the panel's primary and immediate priority, " she said.

She said a separate internal review will be completed by October 1.

Opinion: Can the U.S. Secret Service actually change it ways?

The Washington Post headline read, "**Secret Service Director Resigns After Security Failures**" on the morning of July 16, 1993. Since the Secret Service Director Stephanie Henderson was the first to resigned in the Reid's administration very young first term. Who else will be the next head to roll, roll away and rolled out? The FBI, White House staff and two independent counsels would all have had to agree to assist with the coverup and the list does not include the conspirators in the actual murder of Richard Royster.

o

President Thomas Reid announced unexpectedly on Friday, July 17, 1993 that Chief of Staff John Watkins was quitting and heading home, capping a short and rocky tenure that is expected to last until Election Day in November. Reid's budget director William Murphy, a figure long familiar with Washington's ways and means, it's to take over one of the most time consuming jobs in America.

Watkin's run as Reid's chief manager and gatekeeper lasted only five months. It was filled with consequential moments for the White House, like the murder of White House Counsel Richard Royster, but also stumbles with Congress and grumbles that Watkins was not the right choice to coordinate an intense of ideas, egos and decisions.

Reid said, "he reluctantly accepted the news and at first had refused to accept Watkins resignation letter last week."

Watkin did not waver, expressing to his boss a desire to get back to his family in Memphis, where Reid's have dominated local politics for decades. He offered no explanation on Friday about what accelerated his decision.

It apparently became clear that the fit was no longer working for either side. Senior adviser Jack Rouse already had taken on more of the day-to-day management.

Stepping in is the mild-mannered Murphy, who began began his career as a staffer in Congress, where he spent almost a decade as a principal domestic policy adviser to House Speaker Tip O'Neill. Murphy has worked for Reid as a deputy campaign manager before becoming budget director, the same position he held in the President George Hoover Wilson Burd's administration.

Watkins had been brought in for his political savvy, business ties and experience. Yet as an outsider, despite his vast background with the top political family in Memphis, Reid's hometown. Watkins did not personally know Reid well. That meant he had to figure out the president and run his operation simultaneously. He

o

did not seem to mesh as the one, more than anyone, charged with ensuring a smooth operation.

The President delivered the other side of the story, describing Watkins as highly influential and effective.

"No one in my administration has had to make more important decisions more quickly than John. And that's why I think his decision was difficult for me," Reid said in a State Dining that was nearly empty except for the assembled media.

The mood was decidedly more low-key than other transitions involving the top staff job at the White House.

Reid praised Watkins at length for his help on major decision with the 1992 campaign, the West Wing presidential section had endured private struggles with coordination and communication, particularly with Congress.

Watkins was not pushed out of the door, said a Democratic strategist familiar with the decision. The timing was driven by Watkins personal reflection, yet it also would have become more awkward for the White House had he not left before Reid's tone setting State of the Union, said the strategist, who spoke on condition of anonymity to discuss the personal matter.

The State of the Union speech was held on Jan 26, followed by the release of the White House budget proposal in early February. The chief- of-staff transition is expected to be completed by the end of next month, with Murphy staying on at the Office of Management and Budget until congressional hearings are held on fiscal budget 1994 on Capitol Hill. It is unclear who will lead the agency after that.

Watkins and Murphy stood with the President on Friday but did not speak, The White House said neither man was giving interviews.

Murphy's private sector experience includes a stint as a managing director and chief operating officer of Citigroup's global wealth management division.

o

Watkins, who previously served as co-chairman of Reid's Nashville based election efforts in the 1992 presidential campaign was written into the advance press release given to the media gathered at the State Dining Room announcement.

Unlike Watkins, Murphy comes with deep connections to Congress where Reid's love/hate relationship with lawmakers is a source of constant debate. Watkins's relationship with congressional Democrats was hardly a smooth sailing boat.

Senate Majority Leader Larry Head, the top Democrat in Congress sent out an upbeat statement on Murphy ("a consummate professional with intimate knowledge of Congress") and Watkins (for "handling crises few chiefs of staff have had to face,") .

Robert Gates, a twelve (12) year officer of the Secret Service once defending President Reid with his life, but now say "the billowing fog in the Reid administration" and an inside look at the Commgate scandal led him to turn in his badge, turn on his former boss, and run for Congress as a Republican candidate.

"I was behind the scenes for 12 years at the White House protecting the President. "I have been in the room during some of the most important conversations." Gates told NBCnews.com about the access he had to high level dicussions inside the White House.

Gates' former colleagues are unhappy with him parlaying his proximity to the president into a political career.

"He trying to draw all the attention to himself and he hijacking the Secret Service brand name." agents who had worked with Gates told NBCnews.com. "That's all he's got going for him right now."

Gates, who protected both presidents Reid and George Hoover Wilson Burd, is running for the Republican nomination in Maryland's 6th Congressional District, a seat currently held by Democrat Jason Delaney. The election will be held next year.

o

Gates, 39, is careful not to say too much about exactly what he saw and heard while protecting the president but hints that "It's worse than people really know. They'd be shocked, scared, if they knew everything that is going on."

"Being a Secret Service agent, I have an obligation not to disclose personal conversations and security details," he told NBCnews.com. "But that doesn't prevent from speaking generally about foundational principles and the system of patronage and punishment I saw in the Reid administration."

The defining moment, he says, when he decided to leave the secret service and the enter the field of politics, came after overhearing a series of secret negotiations inside the White House during the past five months.

"If there was one event that helped make up my mind, the most visceral was the universal health care debate. The public doesn't any idea how many deals were cut to try to make it happen but failure to garner enough support among both Democrats and Republicans to enact legislation to become law of the land.
The Republican party has the reputation for being the party of big business, but you wouldn't think that you saw them in the debate. So many people were sold out and so many sold out that it was plain disgusting."'

Gates was Maryland's Republican candidate for Senate in 1991, but lost single handedly to incumbent Senator Dennis Harbin. He is planning on releasing a memoir about his time in the secret service later on this year. Gates said he was "very complimentary of the president and his family." but that the Reid administration had become "enmeshed in so many scandals."

Secret Service agents who served with Gates but asked for anonymity confirmed his resume, but said the candidate "tends to exaggerate his importance on the presidential detail and exaggerate his proximity.

"We don't sit on any meetings at the White House. We don't sit on high-level meetings," the Secret Service agents said.

o

The agents said Gates assignments were "typical of all agents in the president's detail and that he was not a supervisor of the agents.

"Congressman Delaney is focused on serving his consistents and isn't paying much attention to the Republican primary," a spokesman for the Democrat incumbent said in a written statement.

An eventful, interesting week has finally come to an end. Now a typical hot weekend in July begins with concerts, newly released movies and the ever present flock of tourists to Washington, D.C. from around the country and the world. Tourists are fascinated with the world class city that D.C is. I am blessed and fortunate to have grown up here. We are a town that requires living here to understand the many layers of what D.C. is all about. I love DC!

On Monday, July 20, 1993, Attorney General Jamie Woods announced that she will resign after five months at the Justice Department. She has agreed to remain in her post until the confirmation of her successor. 'In the coming months ahead I will leave the Department of Justice." Woods said at the White House, thanking President Thomas Reid for the "greatest honor of my professional life to serve as Attorney General.

Though she is stepping down, Woods said that "she will never leave the work and job entirely."

'I will continue to serve and try to find ways to make our nation better even more true to its founding principles and ideals," she said, without offering any specifics.

Reid stood next to Woods in the White House State Dining Room, praising the first African-American woman to serve as attorney general and who made civil rights and equal rights paramount and central components to her tenure at Justice.

The President noted noted that her department prosecuted hundreds of terror cases, "rooted out corruption and fought violent crime," tackled financial fraud and "attacks on the Voting Rights Act." Reid said Woods also helped to bring the crime rate and incarceration rate by ten percent (10%) over the last five months.

"Jamie has done a superb job, "Reid said, "I just want to say thank you for a job well done."

In a telephone interview with CNN's Devan Perez before the official White House announcement, Woods said she never to stay for the duration of Reid's first term. She said now was the most appropriate time to step down when things are running smoothly at the Justice Department.

"I am confident we're in a good place now, " Woods said, "Now was a good time to go with those accomplishments in the last few months in place."

She stated that protecting voters' right and gay rights, easing federal drug sentencing rules that she argues disproportionately burden minorities and defending the use of criminal courts to try terrorist suspects are critical issues.

"I think I leave on accomplishing a great deal in the specific areas that are of importance to me. "I satisfied with the work we have done in a short period of time," she said.

What will be Jamie Wood's legacy ?

Time will only tell what Jamie Wood's tenure at the Secret Service will be recorded in the agency's history as one of harshness or kindness.

Woods has discussed her plans to step down personally with the President on multiple occasions in recent months in light of Richard Royster's murder, and finalized those plans in a hour-long conversation with Reid at the White House executive residence over the Fourth of July weekend, and Reid administration official said.

Woods duly noted that she has loved the Justice Department since, when she was a little girl, she watched how ---under Attorney General Robert F. Kennedy--the

Justice Department played a dynamic leadership role in advancing the civil rights movement of the 1960's. During her brief tenure as attorney general, Woods has had Kennedy's portrait hung prominently in her conference room.

Woods also has been criticized on several occasions as being overly political, and some Republican members of Congress are shedding few tears over her resignation.

For instance, Rep Jack Graham of South Carolina sent an email to the Justice Department, Good riddance Jamie Woods, Your total disregard for the U.S. Constitution will not be missed."

House Speaker Jay Weems released a similar statement, saying Wood's resignation is "long overdue."

In June 1993, the House voted to hold Woods in contempt of Congress for refusing to turn over documents linked to the murder of Richard Royster.

Upon hearing the news of Wood's resignation, House Oversight Committee Chairman, Rep Dyrol Bossier, who lead the contempt proceedings, called Woods "the most divisive U.S. Attorney in modern history of the Department of Justice."

But Woods has her supporters, including the top Democrat on the Senate Judiciary Committee.

"I particularly appreciate how Attorney General Woods has restored the Civil Rights Division to its historical mission," Sen Edward Parker of Vermont said.

Lawmakers weigh in on Jamie Wood's resignation.

The attorney general's work on the sentencing reforms and efforts to reduce incarceration rates among African-American and Hispanic males.

Those sentiments were echoed by Rep. Mary Williams, chair of the Congressional Black Caucus. She said Wood's departure "will leave a significant void in the Reid administration and in our nation as a whole."

In 1992, Woods described her first meeting with Reid, which occurred just after Reid was elected Governor of Tennessee in 1979.

" I sat next to him at this American Bar Association dinner and we just started talking about a variety of things, sports among them and criminal justice issues. And we saw that we had a lot of similar views and so we just started cultivating a relationship that was casual in nature," Woods said.

Woods was sworn in as the 78th attorney general in January 1993 after serving as President George Hoover Wilson Burd's deputy attorney general, the first African-American to serve in that position.

Previously, the Yale University Law School graduate was U.S. Attorney for the District of Columbia and served during Jerry Brown's administration as an associate judge in the Superior Court of the District of Columbia.

A surprisingly and interesting event occurred on the morning of July 21, 1993 when the Secret Service decide to remove four of its most senior officials while a fifth has decided to retire in what is likely the biggest management shakeup in the agency's 128-year history.

Due to a host of performance. organizational, and technical" failures, an intruder was able to scale the White House fence in June and make his way inside the executive mansion before he was finally taken down by Secret Service agents, according to a report on the incident by the Department of Justice that was made public on Tuesday.

The biggest shakeup in the Secret Service since former Director Stephanie Henderson resigned several weeks ago after a string of security lapses including the murder of White House Counsel Richard Royster in June according to people familiar with the internal discussions.

o

Four senior executives are being demoted in an upper level management after a series of scandals rocking the Secret Service agency, officials said on Tuesday.

The departures would gut much of the Secret Service's upper management, which has been criticized by lawmakers and administrators officials in recent months for fostering a corporate culture of distrust between agency leaders and its rank-and-file, and for making poor decisions that helped erode quality.

The decision was based on the findings of a recent Department of Justice report that outlined the agency's shortcomings, the Secret Service's acting director, Thomas Laramire, said in a statement. The four officials were told of their reassignments immediately.

Laramire, a former leader of George Hoover Wilson Burd's protective detail who took over when Stephanie Henderson resigned as director, told congressional leaders in early July that a desire to fix the distrust of management among both agents and officers was "an integral part of why I agreed to return to duty in the first place."

"Change is necessary to gain a newer, fresh perspective on how we conduct our business," Mr Laramire said. " I am very certain any of four senior executives will be productive and valued assets either in other positions at the Secret Service or the department as a whole."

They were identified as Brandon Morrissey, the assistant director for the Office of Investigations; Doug Dupree, the assistant director for protective operations; Louis Oliver, the assistant director for technology; and June Lawson, the assistant director for government and public affairs. All are eligible to retire from the Secret Service, one official said.

o

The retiring assistant director, Vance Estevez, who had been promoted in 1991 to be assistant director for protection after serving as head of George Hoover Wilson Burd's detail and then named assistant director for training in 1993, announced that he would retire this year in the wake of the panel's findings.

The current changes leave in place at least for the time being the agency's second-in-command manager and one of the longest-serving leaders at the Secret Service: Deputy Director Bernard T. Hughes.

Laramire said that his latest moves were based on the panel's independent review and on "his own assessments of the situation."

The news was first reported by the Washington Post on Monday.

Mr. Laramire who took over the job after the resignation of the director Stephanie Henderson, who resigned under pressure has been remaking the agency's leadership but he has taken no action to address the Department of Justice report said one of the biggest dangers to the president' security: the fence around the White House.

Henderson's resignation came on the very same day the Washington Times reported an armed security guard was in a elevator with President Reid during scheduled April visit to the Centers for Disease Control and Prevention in Atlanta, GA.

No one but law enforcement officers can carry guns in close proximity to the president, and the Secret Service was totally unaware that the man possessed a gun.

The report which was released on July 15 said that the fence must be "changed as soon as humanly possible." It said the fence should be made several feet higher and horizontal bars on it should be replaced with vertical ones to make it more difficult to climb over it. Also, an independent review panel issued a scathing report about the lack of leadership at the agency.

In early June, a man with a knife climbed over the fence in front of the White House's north lawn and managed to get through the North Portico doors and into the East Room before he was tackled down by Secret Service agency officers.

The report noted that members of the agency's Emergency Response Team did not immediately enter the North Portico doors after the intruder had breached the interior because they were familiarized with the layout of the White House.

By the time they entered, the intruder Lou Hernandez had already subdued.

The review also blamed communications failure for the intrusion, noting that several radio and alarm systems to notify Secret Service agents of a breach did not function properly. Perhaps most astounding, the report said that one canine officer who could have conceivably halted Hernandez's mad dash was taking a personal call on his cell phone and did not have his radio earpiece in his ear when Hernandez hopped the White House fence.

Another Secret Service officer who did not see Hernandez approach the White House mistakenly believed the door to the building would be locked as a regular security measure and that Hernandez would be cornered between the door and the approaching agents.

In its review of the White House breach by the fence jumper, the Department of Justice (DOJ) faulted the Secret Service for insufficient training of the officers on duty, nothing that "staffing shortfalls" have left the agency unable to provide regular training for its uniformed division officers. It also noted that the training they did receive did not prepare them for 'non-lethal force scenarios" like the one that unfolded on June 7.

Laramire called the report "a devastating blow to the agency" when he later testified before a congressional panel and promised both immediate action and long term reform of the agency.

o

A few days later a larger comprehensive report was released that concluded that the Secret Service needs more money, more staff, more training, and an outsider at the helm, among other necessary changes to adequately fulfill its core mission of protecting the president.

According to a DOJ spokesman, Adam Ames completed his review on July 15 and a submitted a copy to the Attorney General and to Laramire so the acting director "could immediately begin to take any additional security measures that the findings warranted in order to better ensure the White House complex is secure."

"Acting Director Laramire has already begun to take such measures." the spokesman added.

Ames, according to DOJ, began briefing lawmakers on the report's findings on Tuesday. In reaction to the report, Arkansas Rep. Larry Thompson, the top Democrat on the House Committee on National Security, blasted the "critical and major failures in the areas of communications, confusion about operational protocols, and gaps in staffing and training" factors that contributed to the incident in June.

"While some of these problems can be attributed to a stark lack of resources, others are systemic and indicative of Secret Service culture," he added. Some of these problems have begun to be addressed, however it is imperative that DOJ follow up and through on these findings and institute real reforms."

While much of that report will remain classified, the executive summary that was made public faulted the agency for being too "insular" and concluded that it was "starved for strong leadership that rewards innovation and excellence."

The chairman of the House Judiciary Committee, Rep Bobby Goodbread, to R-Virginia, was less measured in his criticism, slamming the Secret Service for a Shakespearean production of a "comedy of errors" that led to a series of security lapses.

o

"This report makes it perfectly clear that everything that could have gone wrong that evening did," Goodbread said in a statement. "Inadequate training, poor communication. and lax physical security at the White led to this breach."

Goodbread's committee, which holds primary jurisdiction over the Secret Service, is scheduled to hold a hearing on the security breach next month.

Two of Reid's Administration's senior officials on welfare policy resigned today, Wednesday, July 22, 1993 in protest of the law President Reid signed last month ending the Federal guarantee of cash assistance to the nation's poorest children.

The departure of the officials, Emmalee Bradley and Benjamin Rothman, both assistant secretaries at the Department of Health and Human Services, clearly illustrates the continuing deep divisions in the Administration over Mr. Reid's decision to approve the Republican welfare legislation, which the President said he had "serious problems with it" but it was "the best chance we will have for a very long time to complete the work of ending the welfare system as we all know it as."

In a memorandum today to his staff, Mr. Rothman, a longtime friend of the Reids, said "I have devoted my last 30-plus years to doing whatever I could to help in reducing poverty in America. I believe the recently enacted welfare bill goes in the totally opposite direction."

Ms. Bradley, in an email message to colleagues noted that her "deep concerns" about the welfare bill" have led me to conclude that I cannot continue to serve fully" in the job.

Mr. Rothman and Ms. Bradley did not make it clear why they waited until four weeks after Mr. Reid signed the bill, and both declined through spokesman to be interviewed.

Another high ranking official of the department, Philip Smith, quit last month, saying that "to remain would be to disown all the analysis that my office has produced regarding the impact of the bill." Mr. Smith's studies has estimated that the law would push more than a million children into poverty.

The latest resignations came just as the Administration and the states are embarking on a difficult and potentially wrenching effort to move millions of adults from the welfare to work program. The law gives states vast new powers to run their welfare programs with lump sums of Federal money to fund them. It also sets a lifetime limit of five (5) years on benefits to any family and requires most adult recipients to begin working within two years.

Mr. Reid in the past few days has implored churches and businesses alike to use welfare benefits that are given to the states as subsidies to create more jobs for welfare recipients, saying that to make the transition from aid "morally defensible and practically possible, there has to be work for those people to do in the first place."

A large number of state officials attended seminars on the new law in Washington this week and said they were frustrated by their inability to get authoritative interpretations of its provisions from Administration officials.

While the resignations potentially free the Administration to put in a place a team more supportive of the new law, they also deprive the Department of Health and Human Services of great expertise at the very moment when it is needed the most. Ms. Bradley, Assistant Secretary for Children and Families was part of the original team assembled in 1992 to devise his own welfare proposals, and it is her office that will perform the mammoth task of reviewing state plans to carry out the mandates of the new law.

"These are three extremely talented people in the Reid Administration, " said Robert Greenspan, the executive director of the Center for Budget Reform and Policy, a liberal think tank research organization that opposes the welfare law. "I don't there is any question that their departure is a major loss and blow for the Administration,

o

Representative C.C. Jones, III., a Florida Republican who was the driving and primary force behind the welfare bill, also expressed disappointment at the resignations, saying he had held Ms. Bradley" in the highest esteem for her great abilities and honesty."

But Anthony Hughes, a spokesman for Speaker of the House Jack Reynolds, said the crucial question now was "what is the President of the United States is going to do now, not what some assistant secretary of the agency is going to do."

"If he is committed to the rule of law, " he said "he will hire the right people to administer it. If he is not, Daniel Gregg, we know, will enforce the law."

With the resignations to be effective on September 30, the Administration moved quickly to elevate the deputies to Mr. Rothman and Ms. Bradley to be their acting replacements. Officials said that John Olds would be named the Acting Assistant Secretary for Planning and Evaluation, and Cheryl Albright would be named Acting Assistant Secretary for Children and Families.

For Mr. Reid, the resignation of Mr. Rothman was a particular rebuke because he and his wife Margaret Jones Rothman of the Children's First Fund, had been among the Reid's oldest and most loyal supporters in the nation's capitol. Mr. Reid had backed away from nominating Mr. Rothman to an influential appeals of court post and then a lower profile Federal judgeship because of the possibility of a confirmation fight.

And Mrs. Rothman had put increasing public pressure on Mr. Reid not to sign the welfare measure, calling his decision " a critical and crucial moral litmus test of the Reid's Administration."

Officials said that if Debra Y. Soledad remained as the Secretary of Health and Human Services should Reid win a second term in office, the two Acting Assistant Secretaries would be expected to be put forth for Senate confirmation quite easily.

o

Dr. Soledad herself had been a tenacious critic of the welfare bill, but she argued to angry liberals in recent weeks that they need to support Mr. Reid so he could fight for changes in the legislation

" I promise you this, on behalf of the President of the United States," she told delegates at the Democratic National Convention in Cleveland, "that this bill will be changed and that this bill will be improved in years ahead until we get it right for for American families."

Dr. Soledad's spokeswoman, Wendy Coldfield, said the department was making no comment on the resignations. Melody Hooks Banks, a White House spokeswoman said; "The President values their service very much. They have done a terrific job working with helping the children of this country."

As a candidate for President in 1992, Mr. Reid defined himself as a New Age Democratic with his signature pledge to "end the welfare program as we know it." When the President finally announced his own welfare plan in June 1993, it included a two (2) year limit on benefits but coupled it with a $10.3 billion dollar investment over a five year period in an effort to insure jobs creation for people leaving the welfare rolls.

The plan stalled and went nowhere, and after the Republicans won control of Congress in 1992, they quickly seized the initiative on welfare, proposing to give the state's control of welfare policy and trim spending on the program by 45 billion dollars over six (6) years.

Mr. Reid twice vetoed Republican welfare proposals, but this summer he faced a political quandary over whether to risk vetoing another one so close to the election and thus allowing the Republicans to accuse him of breaking his promise to change the welfare system.

His decision to sign the bill created deep fissures in his own party. Senator William Earl Campbell of New York praised Ms. Bradley today.

o

"I told her she had done just the right thing at the right time," Mr. Campbell said in a written statement. "The only people who come back to Washington are the ones who have the sense enough to know when to leave the place. I look forward to her return."

A person who quits a position in any President administration is never an easy thing to do but in a moral sense it is the right thing to do. An individual must hold true to his moral convictions in the times of challenge and controversy.

Charles "Chuck" Reagal eyes his exit of the Reid adminstration on his own terms as detailed in the Washington Post Thursday, July 23, 1993 edition as head of National Security Council.

Chuck Reagal is going out like the he came in: on his own. When the White House invited him to the ceremony in which President Thomas Reid nominated his successor, he did not go or send a representative in his place. As members of Congress scheduled hearings about national security they are getting his successor to be appear on Capitol Hill not him. Wednesday, he expects to stay for several more weeks in the job with an even

And even the White House plans a big, formal farewell for Reagal on next more lower profile. Reagal has always been at arm's length from the White House since his name first leaked as Reid's choice to replace Larry Payne well ahead of his formal nomination keeping him from responding to a concerted opposition campaign.

He made matters even worst with a botched Senate confirmation hearing that members called one of the worst they did ever seen. And he tangled behind the scenes inside the adminstration right up until Reid pushed out early in the year.

Even so, after it all, Reagal is not glum about it, he is very upbeat.

o

He continues to meet with foreign delegations and top commanders,, including the general who is running the administration's effort to begin training and equipping the" moderate "Syrian opposition. On a trip across the country to thank the troops in all four military branches namely Army, Air Force, Marines and Navy, Reagal vowed to work until "the last hour in office," he repeated to each audience assembled that he was proud of his time at the White House.

"I have had a blessed and fortunate life." he told the Marines at Thousands Palm, CA. Later, at the White House, he told reporters how pleased he was to be associated with the finest fighting force in the world.

Reagal's passive approach, his lack of government executive experience and, Lucci said, the almost impossible relationship with the White House meant a whole lot of "muddling along" and little or not much of an imprint on his work at the White House.

Reagals's own camp reject that no notion altogether. It argues there is no question the former Republican senator's "rock steady leadership" and "sweeping reforms " leave national security in better shape than he found it when he took over. And Reagal himself knows he has been the subject and target of alot of Beltway tittering. But as one senior security official put it after Reagal announced his resignation, he remains "sanguine."

At no time on his three day " farewell swing did Reagal allude to the many disputes with the White House that led to his ouster.

"All of the United States of America, I know is extremely proud of the men and women of our armed services." Reagal is quoted in a recent Newsweek article.

"What do I do next? I don't know right now," Reagal mused. "I have not really thought about it. I have never have. I probably shouldn't say this, because I do believe in planning for the future, but I have not thought about my next job. I finish one, and then I think about , well what I could do next? Or how does that all work?... I let the currents take me there.'

o

Reagal has no major regrets about his stint at the White House.

Troops and veterans' advocates have hailed the special attention he has paid to them, including his regular off-the-record lunches to hear it straight from junior enlisted service members. He told troops he is pleased with what he has accomplished, including the necessary reforms of the military health care system and nuclear forces.

All the same, the Reid gridlock meant many other changes that Reagal wanted to make to the national security infrastructure, Department of Defense, or the military, ran into a brick wall like crash test dummies.

That sustained tension with the White House was the real and true source of Reagal's troubles, said a second former senior national security official, who requested not to be identified.

The President wanted someone to be his "puppet" on the National Security Council and ignore right up until world events meant the plan is no longer workable, the official said. When the crises in Syria and Bosnia meant Reid needed a wartime consigliere, Reagal was not prepared to offer a new outlook or perspective. Not only that, by the time the crises were forcing a reluctant administration to change its tack, Reagal also was no longer prepared to just go along to get along.

"I suspect I might not have made everybody here happy always on that point." Reagal acknowledged.

The feeling was mutual.

o

"When he was appointed, they thought he would be the same guy he knew from his days as Tennessee governor and just preside over national security," the former senior defense official said. "They would not prepared for him to develop his own points of view or get in the way as he did on Syria, or with certifying Gitmo detainees for release."

Several of Reagal's predecessors both complained of the level of micromanagement from the White House and senior officials on the National Security Council. Although Reagal has kept mostly silent on the issue, by all accounts, that intense level of scrutiny has persistent.

The former official described a Reagal visit to the Senate to brief then National Security Committee Chairman Mel Stein (D-IL) on the "strategic choices and program management review."

Stein praised the brief. He asked Reagal to send him a copy of the Powerpoint slides he did used. 'Of course I will Senator," Reagal said, But before he even made back to his office inside the White House. Reagal' staff had a got a word from the White House: No, you will not give that Power Point deck of slides to Stein.

"There was a number of things just like this occurring," the official said, "He did not have the full freedom to manage the National Security Council fully as his own."

President Reid praised outgoing National Security Council Director Chuck Reagal on Thursday as " a true American patriot" and "a man from the heartland who devoted his life to duty, honor, country and to America."

"Chuck has helped us prepare for the next century ahead very nicely, " Reid said

o

Reagal, who reportedly announced his resignation in April, thanked the president and dedicated a majority of his remarks to the troops.

"To the men and women who served our country and their families, whose service & daily sacrifice is unequally and unparalleled, you have my deepest appreciation and gratitude," Reagal said.

The President noted that Reagal who was the first enlisted combat veteran and the the first Vietnam veteran to serve as National Security Council Director. Also Reid praised the South Dakota Republican for bringing a bipartisan spirit to national security and defense issues both in the Senate and at the White House.

Mr. Reid also told the gathered audience that he was proud of his proud military service.

Vice President Powell, who also served with Reagal in the Senate and spoke at the ceremony, told him that " you are a man with solid judgment and wise counsel I always sought at for good advice."

Mr. Reagal is expected to leave his post as soon as his expected successor deputy national security official Larry Payne is confirmed by the Senate. Mr. Payne faces Senators for a confirmation hearing next week and his approval could come soon afterwards.

While various news report have cited outgoing tensions between Reagal and Reid's team including National Security Council complaints they were being micromanaged by the White House, officials were all complimentary at the farewell event.

Reid told Reagal that "you have always been very frank" and "said exactly what you had on your mind."

o

"In era of politics that too often transcends into media spectacle, you have always served with decency and dignity." Mr. Reid told Mr. Reagal in a group of hundreds gathered at his farewell ceremony at Joint Base Myer-Henderson Hall on the majestic edge of historic Arlington National Ceremony.

In his farewell address, Mr. Reagal suggested that the United States must resist pressure to rely solely on the military as an absolute solution to complicated global threats.

"We must recognize that there is not an immediate answer to every problem we face with national security, " he said. "Some problems require evolving solutions that gives us the time and the space to adjust, makes adjustments, and the patience to seek higher ground with lasting results."

"Of all the opportunities in my life that has been given me, and I have been blessed with so many. I am most proud of having once been a soldier," said Reagal, who was twice wounded in Vietnam. "The lessons from my time in uniform, about trust, responsibility, duty, judgment, and loyalty to your fellow soldier, these principles that I have carried with me throughout my life."

Outgoing National Security Council Director Chuck Reagal wants to close the U.S. detention center at Guantanamo Bay, Cuba, but he admits it "is going to be difficult task to do."

"This is not a simple, easy matter of just let's just move 166 detainees out of the place," Reagal told National Public Radio(NPR) "Evening Edition" on Thursday. "These people are there for a reason. And as you draw down into the last numbers there, these are the most difficult cases to be undertaken."

In his interview with NPR's Will Smithson, Reagal said he approves the transfer of prisoners only if he is satisfied "that there is substantial mitigation of the risk of these individuals returning to the battlefield to threaten the United States of

o

America or our people or our allies." Reagal added that he had a duty not to formally certify that any detainee could leave the place. "Has there been a slowing of that process, which hasn't always made me popular in some quarters? Yes," Reagal said.

Reagal would only say that "not all people agreed with me on this matter."

"I have made that very clear to the president and to everyone, to the Congress: if it is my responsibility by law, which it is as National Security Council (NSC) Director then I will do everything within my power that I can because the American people rely on me to do so."

When Reagal became NSC director 166 detainees remained inside the facility that was supposed to have been closed years before. During his tenure, Reagal has signed orders to transfer 44 detainees, many of them in recent months. But 122 remain. They remain, Reagal noted, precisely because they have been the most difficult detainees to place elsewhere.

"It is going to be very difficult," Reagal said, "especially if the Congress further restricts where the last 122 detainees can go." Congress has already barred them from being sent to the United States of America. Now that law may change. The Congress is talking about changing the law. So that is job Number 1. If the Congress may do everything, they cannot further inhibit transfers, which they have said, some in Congress, that is what they want to do. We have to find the countries.

The process I have just described to you that we must use in order to, uh move those 122 detainees. So it is going to very difficult to do. So this closing may not happen. "Well, if the Congress throws up roadblocks in disallowing by law any resources for movement and I don't know what else they are going to do, it doesn't make it any easier. It makes it more difficult."

o

Have the White House micromanaged in your experience? Well, every, every president has to find a balance in that position on how he deals with not only his military, but every agency of the government. We in the military, and I put myself in that category since I am National Security Council Director, we have had continue to have every opportunity to express ourselves on every occasion, on every issue. I don't think there is any perfection in the process. It depends on various issues, it depends on the timing, it depends on what is going on at any given time where, as to how much involvement the White House has, wants to have, how much involvement the president has. And again, he is the commander in chief, and the people who work with him at the National Security Council are his arm in working with the Defense Department. And quite frankly, they have responsibility, for all of the government. We are one component of the government."

Have you ever had a moment in the last few months saying to someone at the White House, "Wait a minute, I understand he is the commander in chief , but hold on, you're going too far here"?

"We have had many opportunities to express ourselves on many occasions."

"I just did, Reagal said."

" I have expressed myself in many ways, but I don't get into the book telling business of conversations I have with the president. That is not my style, and I don't think that is a responsible to do.

"When you leave this office, shake hands with Larry Payne, the nominee, if in fact he is confirmed by the Senate, is there a single piece of advice you did give him?" Smithson asked."

"Well, I think, first of all, on Larry Payne, who is superbly qualified to be National Security Council Director with all the jobs he have had here, and he is a friend, has been a friend for many years and was a deputy for a year, a man I greatly admire.

o

He knows this place. He knows the system. So it is different from having someone walk in who hasn't been around this place.

Maybe one thing, he knows this as well, but one thing that I would emphasize is listen. Listen, listen, listen, and I am not sure leaders listen enough, especially to their people. And I have always thought in everything I tried to do in my life, in the jobs I have had, is that if we can turn our transmitters off and our receivers on more often, we are better leaders and we know more of what is going on and therefore we can lead more effectively.

But we can lead with everybody being part of it. No one person leads alone, cannot do it, it is virtually impossible. You need a team, especially in this place."

"Were you ever listened while you was at the White House?" said, Smithson

"Well, all I can do is present what I think is the best interest of this country and how I can best serve this country and the president of the United States of America. And I feel very good about that opportunity I have had."

"You did not say you were listened to, though." Smithson mused.

Reagal responded, " Well Yes, I was listened to, for sure."

Smithson said, "Thank very much National Security Council Director Reagal for satting down with me for this interview."

Reagal said, "Thank you."

The onslaught of White House continues on into the following week.

Peterson and Paulson will leave major vacancies in the West Wing of the White House as Reid looks to the next three years of his young administration. Reid will now need to recruit new staffers to come on board if he hopes to run for a second term of office in 1996.

o

"While their departures are significant, there is indeed value in bringing in new energized staff with fresh ideas and new perspectives," a White House official said, noting Paulson and Peterson had made their decisions to leave independent from one another.

"Instead of filling jobs as one-offs, this timing presents an great opportunity to build a cohesive team that is expressly designed to achieve and implement the President's priorities for the first quarter of his presidency," one White House official said.

Peterson is one of the longest-serving Reid's staffers, with ties to the President's presidential campaign in 1991. A previous White House communications director, Peterson serves as an assistant to the President and senior adviser-- a role he is used to hone the administration's internet presence in a shifting media environment.

"Brian has been beside me on every step of this incredible journey, starting with those earliest days of the campaign back in 1991," Reid said in a statement on Monday morning of July 25. 1993 "And through it all, he has been smart, steady, tireless and true to the values we started with accountability, responsibility and transparency."

An official at the White House said Peterson, who had been contemplating leaving the adminstration " since the inauguration back in January." told Reid the day after the inaugural address that he had made his decision to depart.

"Given the position of strength we are in right now… he is comfortable with ns moving on," the official said.

Paulson who also served in former President George Hoover Wilson Burd's adminstration is expected to assume a role on his son's Gregory Burd's campaign, should he decide to run. Two reliable sources familiar with the campaign's

o

planning said Paulson was likely to take on the top position as communications director.

She will joining another former Reid adviser, Daniel Gray, who is also expected to assume a major role on Burd's campaign, potentially as its chairman. A top aide who helmed the administration's efforts on healthcare for all Americans, Gray is slated to leave the White House this month.

As one of Peterson's final tasks at the White House, he reviewing plans for redesigning the White House's web site. The White House official said Peterson had traveled to Silicon Valley recently to garner recommendations from American high tech firms on how best to engage audiences using the internet to keep the American public update with adminstration events and happenings.

In an interview on CNN's "Reliable Sources" in January, Peterson said his White House position "has been the greatest job I have ever had."

However, he acknowledged "there will be a day when it makes sense for me to do something else in my life," but he said he had not made up his mind about what is next.

"I think when I leave the White House, whenever that will be, I will spend a significant amount of time on a white sandy beach with an adult beverage for a long time," he said with a huge laugh. "And then figure out what the next chapter is."

In January, Peterson spoke animatedly about American media being "on slippery slope and cusp of a massively disruptive ,revolution."

"There are new big things that are going to happen," he said. "The old models are starting to fall away. And how we adjust to them-- you know, entertainment television, the movies, the news, politicians and the government trying to get their message out--- is going to be a massively fascinating thing."

o

Peterson added that he thinks these changes are "even more interesting and potentially consequential than the invention of television and the invention of the Internet, because it is all those things combined together at the same time."

Peterson's departure leaves few remaining "Reid's originals"--- those trusted aides and advisers who helped Reid win the White House and navigate his presidency Jessica Lyons and Bonita French Alexis, both senior advisers who have served Reid for years back when he was governor of Tennessee, are the two trusted aides who will remain in the West Wing of the White House.

Others, however have moved on: Dennis Bryant, Dennis Biddle and Robin Lawrence, three former senior advisers who served on Reid's 1992 campaign, have all left government service for now.

Reid said Monday that Peterson had served not only as a top but as a friend as well.

"I am going to really miss having him around just down the hall from me in the Oval Office," he said.

Also Reid said, "It is like losing a member of your family when he leaves here."

White House staff upheaval is actually quite normal, says former Burd, McLean Adminstration Officials.

For President Reid, 1993 has been a year of goodbyes at the White House. The loss of those key players --who have both served under Reid's presidency as well as his campaign for president comes after the other transitions in the administration's

o

highest ranks including the death of White House Counsel Richard Royster last month.

To the casual observer, and perhaps to the delight of Reid's critics, the staff departures may suggest a White House engulfed in a pit of chaos. The Reid adminstration has certainly been on the defensive side a whole lot lately, scrambling to security problems within the United States Secret Service, fighting to keep a focus on success of the president's agenda.

"Either you have fulfilled what you can contribute to the overall agenda, you are just pure and simple tired, or financially you cannot afford to do it anymore. Or the president can no longer be confident that you are the best person for the job." said Blanche Lincoln, former chief of staff to the first lady and special assistant for White House Management under President George Hoover Wilson Burd

Also Lincoln said," what the president needs at this stage of the game is a clear sense of people prepared to stick around for the long haul to the bitter end."

"You really do not want to make a lot of changes in your first year in office, if you can help it," Lincoln said.

Bert Westheimer, President George H.W. Burd's press secretary from January 1989 to July 1991, said Reid's staff exodus does not mean the White House is in a disarray. On the contrary, he said, "it means people are making wise decisions, both personally and professionally to move on with their lives."

"The White House is not like the Hotel California movie." Westheimer said, "You are allowed to leave the White House and it is healthy and a good thing for the president if the staff does turn over a bit."

"The overall goal is not to stick around forever at the White House because that leaves people too battle hardened," Westheimer said, he compared the White House turnover with a relay track race, where the baton is passed, but never dropped. The

o

real key to maintaining successful White House staff shop is for one person to slow down as another person speeds up and smoothly takes over. Not that everyone does that.

"If anything people in the Burd adminstration probably stayed too long and lost a little bit of their mental sharpness without realizing it," Westheimer said.

In the case of Reid's latest departures, some had already stayed longer than they had initially planned. Blumenthal had envisioned leaving at the end of 1992, but stuck around a little bit longer at the president's request. Kevin Richards took over as Reid's press secretary on February 1993 and thought that he would keep the job for three years. In the end result Richards said "it was not burnout that fueled his decision to resign, It was to spend more time with his kids.

"To live the familiar cliche, If I was single or married but with no kids, I don't think that there is any question in my mind that I would go to the end of the term." Richards said, " I love my job and there is never going to be another experience that I am likely to have that is remotely similar. But I think that as much as I tried to carve out some quality time for my kids, there is still, you still miss a lot."

The process of leaving a top White House position is not simple as giving a two weeks notice in most normal jobs. First of all, it involves telling the president you won't be working for him or her any longer. Secondly, The White House chief of staff communicates the changes to the senior staff members and plots target dates for the transition and a successor to take over. Finally, another team manages the public perception and puts together talking points to help shape the transition period. All of this is kept under wraps, meanwhile, with extreme care to avoid a media circus or frenzy so prevalent in Washington life.

In Richard's case, he said his own team "was mindful of the fact that they planned to announced his resignation at the onset of Richard Royster' death and the security breaches by the Secret Service. The White House decided that the afternoon of July 25 was the best window to slip in Richard's announcement.

o

"Monday, after the events of the morning, made a lot of good sense, " Richards said, "If you wait for the perfect time to do almost anything here, you are going to waiting forever and a day."

And for many people, that breaking point traces it way back to the very people who are sacrificing in their personal lives. A White House official said.

"It is not surprising to see so many people leaving the White House now, since people are bound to hit their natural breaking points at this initial stage in the presidency." said one White House official.

"Once the train has left the station, there is nothing you can do about, " Westheimer said. "The person could come back as the resurrected Jesus Christ. It is not going to change the situation upon their leaving."

"I don't think it has anything to do with a post presidential election year as much as it does the time-honored Washington tradition that people demand the scalp-- and the more senior, the better--when something goes wrong," Westheimer said. "It does not necessarily solve the whole problem, but it gets through the day, unless you are the scalp one."

Dissent from Democrats does play a role, Westheimer added, given to a larger extent a big part of Reid's playbook has been to blame the Republicans for politicizing controversies.

"Well, that doesn't hold up the people criticizing you are Democrats themselves." Westheimer said. "And that is what the Richard Royster's murder non-survivable."

The Washington Post headline on the morning of Tuesday, July 26, 1993 read
Larry Payne Wins Senate Approval as National Security Council Director

o

The United States Senate on Monday confirmed Larry Payne to be the next National Security Council (NSC) Director, installing a new NSC chief as the United States increased military action against Syria.

Mr. Payne, a former deputy assistant director who is President's Reid's choice to replace Chuck Reagal, was approved by a vote of 95 to 3.

The transition to a new NSC chief comes as Congress considers a number of national security issues, including a draft request by Mr. Reid that would formally authorize military action against the terrorist threats in Syria. Many lawmakers expressed reservations about the parameters of the authorization regarding the use of ground troops and its place with an existing authorization of military action.

Senator Gregory T. Kirkland, Republican of Ohio, who voted Mr. Payne, said, "Mine is a vote of no confidence in the national security decisions of the Reid adminstration."

Senator Benjamin LittleJohn, Republican of Arizona and the chairman of the Armed Services Committee, called Mr. Payne "one of America's most experienced national security professionals." But he said he did not think Mr. Reid would put his full and confidence in Mr. Payne.

Payne will also inherit an air war in the Middle East, tensions in Bosnia, Croatia and Russia. The U.S. led bombing campaign against militants in Syria started in February and continues with more than 630 million dollars spent.

Payne has worked under 5 NSC Directors, including the last three, and owns a doctorate in engineering. He is "extremely adept at juggling complex problems, said Alexander Simms, who was Lewis Arnetta's chief of staff at the CIA and Pentagon.

From Day One, Payne will have to deal with a possible threat of sequestration automatic cuts to the National Security budget set for October 1. The Joint Chiefs of Staff warned senators last week that reductions, which affect every facet of the programs but troops' compensation could prevent the military from winning a war against a determined enemy and threat to national security.

"If we go back to sequestration, I think we are all in trouble, to be quite frank about it," Reagal said. "There may be a dumb and dumber way to cut the huge defense budget, but I cannot think of one. Because you are basically cutting the least important thing that you do and the most important thing that you do by the same amount."

"The result of sequestration is those programs for our military families and wounded warriors are now being cut at the same rate as the dumbest thing the department of Defense does," Reagal said. "It is a travesty of sensible management and responsibility."

Reid has called for an end to the sequestration, which would reduce military spending by $1 trillion dollars over a ten (10) year period. He will need cooperation from the Republican-led Congress to make it happen.

In March, Reagal and Arnetta's appearing at a national security conference, complained about meddling in military affairs by White House staffers. Arnetta talked about military decisions being made without adequate input from the Pentagon.

Simms, who is advising Payne, dismissed concerns about White House staffers interference affecting Payne. Simms noted that Payne was chosen by President Reid to be Arnetta's deputy and has known Debra Gray, the defense adviser, for years.

"He will not hesitate to pick up the telephone and call the White House if he has a concern," Simms said.

"The major difference is that Payne has served for more than five years in two administrations", Reagal said, "So he know this president; this president knows him. He knows all the principal players at multiple levels. They will be very familiar to him, and he to them. That will make a big difference in terms of working relationships."

"Payne's ties to the White House should serve him well, Reagal said."

Simms and Reagal also stressed Payne's strong commitment to getting troops the proper gear they need to survive in battle situations. Payne as deputy NSC director, helped shepherded efforts to speed up specially designed Mine Resistant Ambush Protected (MRAP) trucks to Afghanistan for protection against homemade bombs. He also took an special interest in fielding bomb sniffing dogs to keep trucks on foot from stepping on bobby traps.

In several interviews dating back to 1988, Payne came across very focused and voluble. He would hold forth on training Labrador retrievers for combat and keeping assembly lines humming for MRAPS. Grant, an attack helicopter pilot with combat commands in both Iraq and Afghanistan, was a regular presence as a military adviser to Payne.

Payne has a a few critics in Washington, including the Group on Government Oversight and Accountability, a non-partisan, good government project group. They note that Payne has worked as a defense industry consultant between his NSC jobs and also served on boards that advised the government on policies with potential to benefit his clients, such as Aerospace, a major contractor.

Payne's potential conflicts of interest was raised at his congressional confirmation hearing, said Richard Smalls, an investigator for the organization, "That was not a major issue for him to huddle over at all," Small said.

CHAPTER FIVE
REQUIEM

-the requiem how be sung "By you-by yours, the evil eye,-by yours, the slanderous tongue" That did to death the innocent that died, and died so young?
Poems by Edgar Allan Poe

According to Merriam Webster Requiem is defined as a mass said or sung for the repose of a departed soul. In this case bode well in the developments of our story, we are referring to the departed soul of White House Counsel Richard Royster who passed on the Great Beyond last month. With the torrendous week of staff departures, Michael Cradle was active on the case.

o

One a clear and balmy day of July 26, Cradle is meeting with his Chief of Detectives at 9:00 a.m.

"How long you figure that this continue to go on?" Chief asked.

"What, this case?" Cradle responded.

"Yeah, and everything that goes along with it. You got a good deal here." Chief said.

"I like these high profile cases to be solved." "To answer your question, I plan to wrap it up in a next couple of days." Cradle said.

"Alright Mike, I will hold you to this." "Maybe the killer does not wants to be found." Chief replied.

"I am not following you." Cradle said.

"Why else would a murderer lay low? People who get murdered makes their families feel guilty somehow. Like they were victims or all at fault in other words, you know what mean? You got any better answers?" Chief said.
"No I don't Sir." Cradle replied.

Then, Cradle walks out of his Chief's office back to his own office. As he crosses the threshold, the telephone rings with an unfamiliar voice on the other end with a British accent.

"Hello, Detective Michael Cradle, It's Inspector Edward Windsor of the New Scotland Yard."
"I saw your murder suspect posting on INTERPOL's website via your Federal Bureau of Investigation."

INTERPOL is the largest international police organization with 190 member countries founded in 1914 at the first international Criminal Police Congress held

o

in Monaco. Officially created in 1923 as the International Criminal Police Commission, the Organization known as INTERPOL in 1956. It's role is to enable police around the world to work together to make the world a safer place.

INTERPOL's high tech infrastructure of both technical and operational support helps meet the growing challenges of fighting crime. The General Secretariat is located in Lyon, France and operates 24 hours a day 365 days a year.

INTERPOL has also seven regional offices across the world and a representative office at the United Nations in New York. Each of the 190 countries maintains a National Central Bureau staffed by its own highly trained law enforcement officials.

Transnational crime cannot be tackled in isolation anymore, its reach is wider than traditional law enforcement. Partnerships with other organizations and the private and public sectors are essential to tackle challenges in common areas as well.

While the vision and mission of INTERPOL remain in line with the original goals of the meeting in 1914, the Organization continues to evolve in response to the needs of its member countries, the emergence of new crime waves, trends and innovative in technology.

"Inspector Windsor, Do you have any leads for me in the case," Cradle asked.

"Yes, I do. the murderer was spotted here in London a day or two ago," Inspector Windsor responded.

"Thank Inspector Windsor for calling me to share this information with me." Cradle said.

"We here at the New Scotland Yard are happy to assist our American counterparts in bringing fugitives to justice." Inspector Windsor

"Inspector Windsor, I will see you in London very soon." Cradle said.

o

Cradle hangs the phone with a brimming grin. "He says to himself I always wanted to go to London."

Talking out loud, "I guess I need to get a bowler hat, and I will be right at home in London."

Now, he walks down the hallway to his Chief's office to inform him of his pending trip to London.

"Chief, I got a new lead on the Royster's murderer being seen in London via a phone call from Scotland Yard." Cradle said.

"Mike, I guess you will leaving for London today." Chief said.

" I getting over to London as quickly as possible and see if I can track him down." Cradle said.

" When do you plan to leave?" Chief responded.
" I am leaving this afternoon for London Sir." Cradle said.

"Alright Mike, I will see you in a few days for a full report on your trip." Chief said.

"Thanks Chief, I will see you soon." Cradle said.

Cradle walks back down the hall to his office to wrap up things for the day. He shuts off his computer and locks his desk since he will be gone for several days in London.

He proceeds to shutoffs the ceiling light in his office and desk lamp in his office as well on his way out with the Richard Royster's case file in his portfolio. Then, he catches the elevator down stairs of MPD headquarters, walks out of the backdoor to get into his Ford Crown Victoria parked on the street on a slant with the other detective's car parked as well.

o

He drives from 3rd and C Streets NW and merges onto I- 395 South, Take exit 7 on the left towards I-295 South, keeping left towards I-295 South. Exiting left to merge onto I-295 South towards I-95, I-395. Continuing on Indian Head Highway. Keeping left on I-95 North towards Baltimore. Next, taking exit towards Indian Head MD 210, keeping left on Indian Head Highway, turning right onto Old Fort Road. At the end of the road, he turns left onto Fort Washington Road and makes another left onto Warburton Drive.

Cradle drives up to his driveway and parks his car there. He rushes into his house to start packing immediately for his trip to London. Then, he decides to get a Blue Shuttle to Dulles International Airport instead of driving his own car and leaving it parked in a lot for several days with fees being upwards of $25.00 per day for each day it is parked there.

Cradle finishing packing his roller duffle bag, next places a call to the Blue Shuttle for pick-up for Dulles.

Cradle: "I would like to schedule a shuttle pick-up for Fort Washington, MD to Dulles Airport. British Airways gate please"
Dispatcher: "I can schedule you for pick-up Sir from your home to Dulles in 30 minutes."
Cradle: "How much will it cost?"
Dispatcher: "It will be $30.00"
Cradle: "That is very reasonable, Go right ahead and book it."
Dispatcher: "Great, How do you want to pay for it Mastercard, Visa or American Express?"
Cradle: "I will give you a Visa, here is my number 4156 3420 2081 2873 Exp Michael G. Cradle 02/1995"
Dispatcher:"Thank you Sir, You are approved." "Your shuttle will be there in 30 minutes."

Cradle hangs up the phone with Blue Shuttle, he starts the arduous task of packing for his overseas to London to track down the sightings of Richard Royster's murder there. He goes to his upstairs closet and pulls out his Ralph Lauren leather duffel bag that was a gift from his son and daughter from Father;s Day last month.

He hurriedly packs shirts, slacks, ties,shoes and toiletries in the duffle bag. Enough clothes that he will need for a few days out of the country. It is now 2:30 pm and the shuttle should be arriving promptly at 4:00 p.m. Time is of essence. He calls up a neighbor next door to ask them to watch his house for a few days. Now, he see the Blue Shuttle heading the down the street towards his house.

Then, he proceeds to hang up the phone with his next door neighbor and rushes downstairs to his front door as the driver proceeds to blows his horn to announce he is there to pick him up.

The driver see him running towards him to board the shuttle and get out to open up the backdoor of the shuttle for which Cradle can store luggage on his trip out to Dulles International Airport.

Driver: "Good afternoon Mr. Cradle, now allow me to open the door for you."
Cradle: "Thank you Sir."

Cradle boards the shuttle and the driver speeds off en route to Dulles. It is a hot and humid afternoon in the DC Metropolitan area, so the shuttle driver has his air conditioner to the maximum level for Cradle's comfort.

Driver is bustling down 210 towards the exit for the Wilson Bridge. The traffic across the bridge is free flowing and no backups as he heads towards the famous mixing bowl in Springfield, Virginia in a matter of minutes. Now, as the shuttle gets closer to Tyson Corner and moves slower in the clogged inner loop of Beltway 495 rush hour traffic. The snarled traffic does not last long as the shuttle whisks towards the exit for the Dulles Toll Road. The time is only 5:00 p.m. now and Cradle will be able to catch an evening flight to London.

o

A few minutes later, the Blue Shuttle is pulling up to the British Airways gate. Cradle gets out of the shuttle, grabs his rolling Ralph Lauren[duffle bag from the rear of the shuttle with the assistance of the driver.

Michael Cradles proceeds towards the British Airways ticket counter. The female ticket agent greets him with a smile.

"How may I help you Sir." She replied.

"I would like to purchase a round trip to London with a return date of July 30." Cradle said.

"Okay Sir, I have a 6:30 p.m. flight to London." She said.

"That works for me." Cradle answered.

"The round trip ticket will cost $847.00" She said.

"Fine, here is my credit card and ID. Also, I am a DC Metropolitan Police Detective on a special assignment."

"Detective Cradle is your tickets for your flight." She responded.

"Thank you." Cradle said.

"Would you like to check any luggage." She asked.

"No, I only have this one, a roller duffle bag." Cradle said.

"One more thing Detective Cradle just let airport security know that you are a law enforcement officer, so they can store your gun in a firearms container for your flight over to London." She told him.

"Alright Ms, you have been very helpful. Thank you." Cradle replied.

o

Cradle leaves the British Airways ticket counter with his tickets coupled with his Ralph Lauren roller duffle bag.

Michael Cradle retrieves his .22 revolver from Security at London's Heathrow Airport. He was licensed to carry the weapon, and had to checked with airline security at Dulles before boarding the flight.

The revolver securely nestled beneath while rolling his Ralph Lauren roller duffle bag, he proceeds over to Customs where he presents his passport and places his duffle bag on the table for their inspection.

He informs the customs officials that he is a law enforcement from Washington, DC and will be in London on official business for (3) three days.
One custom officer responds "You are free to go Detective Cradle, enjoy your stay in London."

Cradle responds, "Thank you."

Now he walks out front of the airport to take a shuttle bus to pick up the Hertz Lincoln Continental he did reserved for three days.

"Very nice, very nice," he said aloud as he settled behind the Lincoln's steering wheel and adjusted his seat and mirrors. He places a call on his cell phone to Edward Windsor at the New Scotland Yard to let him know he is in town.

"Hello Inspector Windsor, It is Detective Michael Cradle from Washington, DC we spoke on the phone a day or so ago , Now, I am here in London."

"Great to hear Detective,Would you like to come over to NEW Scotland Yard to meet with me." Inspector Windsor said.

o

"Sure I would like to meet with you regarding the sighting of the murderer here." Cradle responded.

"Alright Detective Cradle, I will give you our address 10 Broadway close to St. James Park tube station in the borough of Westminster." Inspector Windsor said.

"Thanks Inspector Windsor, I will be right over in my rental car after put your address in my Global Positioning System (GPS) in the car ." Cradle said.

Cradle inputted the New Scotland address in his GPS which up on the small screen as 8.2 miles from Heathrow which is a 21 minutes drive. He took the exit roundabout onto Swansea Road, a slight left turn onto Great Southwest Road and driving 2.4 miles at the roundabout, he takes the third exit onto Bath Road. Proceeds to drive 3.9 miles onto Windmill Road as he goes down to the end of the road turning right onto Windmill Road until he reaches the end of the road again and turns left onto Northfield Avenue.

He drives another 1.1 miles, turning left onto Kim Road, going 128 feet until at end of the road and turning left onto Kitchen in which he sees the tall windowed building on the right.

He parked across the street from 10 Broadway, got out of the Lincoln, spent a moment to take in his surroundings, then crossed the street in which he spots the famous revolving New Scotland Yard sign

He runs to the corner, crossed, slowly walking towards the New Scotland building. Cradles enters the lobby of the building, flashes his DC Metropolitan Police Detective badge along with his passport to the boobies on post at the entrance. The boobies motions him onto to the metal detector as it immediately sounds off. No big deal, No reason for an alarm since he is sworn officer of law enforcement just like them.

o

Inspector Windsor is already down in the lobby area waiting on for Michael Cradle to arrive. Windsor is a tall, slim man with mixed gray hair wearing round glasses.

Windsor flashed his biggest nonthreatening smile. "I presume, you are Detective Michael Cradle from Washington, D.C."

"Michael Cradle," he said, extending his hand

"A pleasure to finally meet you, Detective Cradle. I am Inspector Edward Windsor."

"Great" Cradle replied.

" I will take you upstairs to my office." Inspector Windsor said.

They walk over to the bank of elevators, proceed to take the one up to the sixteenth (16) floor. A relatively fast elevator ride.

A few minutes later, Cradle and Windsor are seated in a large office. The walls are covered with plaques, framed newspaper clippings and photographs with prominent people such as Queen Elizabeth II, prime ministers and heads of states.

"Fond memories" Inspector Windsor said from where he sit in a huge leather chair on an oak panelled desk.

"You are a star huh?" Cradle said.

"No, never a star just a good damn investigator and gumshoe detective." Inspector Windsor responded passionately.

Cradle glance over at him and his vast wall of achievements "I am very impressed with your illustrious career here at the New Scotland Yard."

o

"Thank you, Detective Cradle, I am confident that you are my equal with just as many awards and mementos." Inspector Windsor.

"You are welcome." Cradle said.

"The killer of Richard Royster was last spotted right here in London at Harrod's " Inspector Windsor said.

"Thanks for the information, Inspector Windsor." Cradle replied.

" Where are you staying Detective Cradle." He asked.

"I will be staying a hotel called Claridge on 38 Davies Street." Cradle responded.

"Maybe we can have lunch or dinner while you are in town," Inspector Windsor said.

"Great, Let's make it tomorrow night," Cradle said lightly.

"Dinner, is just fine with me." Inspector Windsor replied.

Windsor escorts Cradle out of his office, shakes hands and leaves him to catch his elevator back downstairs to the lobby area. As he walks out of the door, a London shower occurs, so he uses his suit coat to cover his head from the rain. He anxiously waits for the light to change, so he can run quickly to his Lincoln parked across the street.

He gets into the Lincoln and speeds away over to the Claridge where he is staying. Cradle takes a left onto 30 Davies Street , then he parks his Lincoln in a space directly in front of the Claridge He gets out of his car, retrieves his duffle bag from the trunk and enters into the revolving door of the Claridge main entrance.

He stops at the front desk to check in.

o

'I am Michael Cradle checking in." The hotel clerk responds, "I will look your reservation up in our system."

"Yes, Yes, I got it." She said.

"Alright" Cradle responds.
"Michael Cradle for a three (3) nights stay. She said.

"Please sign the reservation card Mr. Cradle." She said.

He completes signing it.

"Thank you Sir." She said.

"You are welcome Ms." Cradle said.

"Here is your cardkey to the room, Do you need a second a key?" She said.

"No one key is just fine." Cradle replies.

"Alright Sir." She said.

"Thank you." Cradle said.

The lobby area was half filled with men and women enjoying cocktails while a tuxedoed pianist played some show tunes.

The music enticed weary travelers strolling by in which Cradle was in that majority today due to the long flight from DC earlier.

Cradle lingered a few second more taking in the ambience of the hotel lobby and the lovely upbeat music.

Anyway, this Claridge Hotel is some classy joint. They gave a pair of slipper and a robe. Ciao!

o

Then, he catched a near by elevator to his room on the seventh (7) floor. He proceeds to walk towards his room numbered 706, slide his card key and steps into his room. He turned on a table light on from the wall switch and quickly surveyed the room, which presented him with nothing of immediate interest. The drapes were drawn across the windows of the hotel, he places his Ralph Lauren duffle bag down on the suitcase rack at the foot of the bed.

At the end of his first day in London, Cradle ordered up a bucket of ice, bottles of vodka and scotch, and two club sandwiches. He stripped off his traveling clothes, took a hot shower, turned on the television, and poured himself a drink. Since he was off duty it was perfectly okay for him to have a drink in his room. He took halfhearted bite from one of the sandwiches, took sip from his scotch on the rocks and watched some television.

Cradle yawns loudly now overcome totally by jet lag and immediately stretches out tired body on the oversize king size bed falls fast asleep

Cradle body's have had to adjust to the six (6) hours time difference between London and DC. He wakes up at 6:30 am like clockwork. He takes a morning shower, gets dressed, picks up the telephone and , dialed the telephone for the front desk. He places an order for a full English breakfast shown in the hotel menu and to find out what time does Harrod's open for business. The desk clerks tells Cradle that Harrod's opens at 10:00 a.m. and his breakfast will be brought up in thirty (30) minutes.

A Full English is brought up consisting orange juice, cereals, stewed or fresh fruits but the heart of the Full breakfast is bacon and eggs, Accompanied by sausages, grilled tomato, mushrooms, tea, toast and marmalade.

Cradle took his time finishing breakfast since it was only 8:00 am. Harrod's would not be open until another 2 hours from now. He had time to review his Richard Royster murder case file and to read the latest edition of both the London Times and the Washington Post left outside of his hotel room door. He even turns on the

o

television set in his room to Sportscenter to catch up on the NFL training camps especially with the Washington Redskins in which he was a fan.

An hour late, he leaves his hotel, takes the elevator down to the lobby and walks out of the main entrance. The valet has brought up the Lincoln from the hotel garage. A nice and clear day in London. He steps out into the driveway, tips the valet and get into the Lincoln and programs his GPS to Harrods 87-135 Brompton Road Knightsbridge London.

He turns right onto New Bond Street, then another right onto Bruton Street and down Burton for a tenth of a mile and turning left onto Berkeley Square. Turning right onto Berkeley Square ,makes left onto Fitzmaurice Place traveling down to end of the road then turning right onto Curzon Street and a slight left turn onto Bolton Street and end of the road turning right onto Piccadilly. Now going eight tenths of a mile keeping left and he sees the famous Harrods on the left. It is only 9:20 and the store opens at 10. Cradle parks his Lincoln and waits patiently hopefully to see Richard Royster's killer enter Harrods this morning.

The successful Harrods in London was founded by Charles Henry Harrod in 1834 where began selling groceries in Stepney. In the 1840s, he rented a small shop on Brompton Road, Knightsbridge, know as "Harrods." The shop sold groceries and only had a turn of 20 pounds per week. Upon his retirement in 1860 Charles sold the business to his son, Charles Digby Harrod. The trade at Harrods continued to grow and by 1868 the shop had sixteen (16) staff and the turnover had risen to 1,000 pounds per week. Harrod concentrated on encouraging wealthy people to his store and provided personalized service for very important customers. He also managed to increase trade by introducing his own band groceries patriotically packaged in the colors of the Union Jack flag.

As Cradle waits for the killer to arrive at Harrods, he turns on his car radio to BBC news and the newscaster reports "US President Reid to Visit UK in September"

o

He thinks to himself that his case should be wrapped up before then and be safely back at home in Washington. In order to kill some time, he dialed his cell phone to Inspector Windsor's office. A few minutes later, Windsor was on the line.

"This is Detective Cradle."
"What are you doing."
" I am staking out here over at Harrods for the killer."
"That is great to hear Detective, I hope he shows up soon."
"Inspector Windsor I will have to cancel our dinner meeting due for tonight, my plan to follow this killer like white on rice."
"Okay, no problem Detective, you will get back to London someday before I retire from Scotland Yard."
"Thank again Inspector Windsor for all your great help and assistance."

Cradle hangs out the phone with new found friend here in London. He see a silver Aston Martin pulls and parks directly out front of Harrods. A dark shady figure gets out of the car, what appeared to be a man in an Abercrombie & Fitch baseball cap with "AF" insignia on the front of it.

Cradle observed her closely through his binoculars. She took that cap off, and shaked her long red flowing hair in the wind. Her hair had been curled and redyed, less black showing at the roots.

Her nails had been done, and her makeup was heavy enough to border on the outlandish. Purple eye shadow flecked with gold sparkles covers broad, swollen eyelids, and the weight of long black false lashes threatened to pull her eyes closed at the moment.

Her lipstick was fiery red as her nails, and she did created too large a mouth with it. Pendulous gold plated earrings hung from the lobes of her ears to her broad shoulders and multiple strands of costume jewelry ringed her neck.

She walk into the main entrance of Harrods carrying the green shopping bag given to the shoppers of Harrods. While the killer is inside of Harrods. Meanwhile,

o

Cradle hops out of his Lincoln, heads over to the Aston Martin and plants a small tracking device underneath of the killer's vehicle. The task has been Cradle get back into his parked Lincoln and waits for her to come out of the store.

A few minutes transpired, she walks out the front door carrying Harrods green bag with her purchased goods in it. It appears to be fairly heavy she struggles to carry as Cradle watches from his Lincoln.

She opens the trunk of the Aston Martin and places the Harrods shopping bag in it. Slams the trunk and gets into the driver' seat and speeds in the clear sunny morning. The tracking device is activated remotely by Cradle driving along in his Lincoln. The killer drives away unaware that Cradle is following along her every move at this point. She turns left onto Upper Brook Street instead of a right for some reason.

Now traffic is a standstill due to an overturned truck has spilled fresh all over the road. Cradle is totally disgusted even more so, since he was tracking the killer so relentlessly. A bloody mess a typical British citizen would say of the matter.

The killer has arrived at the fabulous Claridge hotel, parks the Aston Martin in front, walks into the main entrance and approaches the front desk clerk. She tells him that her husband is staying here and that she wants to surprise him. Also, she orders a fresh pot of coffee to be sent up to the room. The front desk clerk obliges her and gives her card key for 706 which is Michael Cradle's room.

She takes an elevator from the hotel lobby to the seventh (7) floor and proceeds down the hallway to Cradle's room marked 706 on the door.

The killer slides the card key and it turns green giving her access to his room. She noticed remnants of the full English breakfast that Cradle had eaten several hours ago.

o

A loud knock at the door, "Room service" porter said. She hurriedly open the door and exchanges the cold pot of coffee with the new fresh, hot pot of coffee and he leaves with it. She quickly closes the door and goes to work. The fresh pot of coffee is placed on the table in the exact location as the previous one.

She removes a small vial of liquid from her Louis Vuitton purse and pours the entire vial of a substance in the nice hot pot of coffee. She figures that Cradle will be knocked out for several hours and she can make her quick getaway from London to Paris.

A few minutes later, she leaves Cradle room, catches the elevator back down to the lobby and turns the card key back into the front desk clerk. She slides him a tip of $20.00 USD and exits out of the main entrance. "Thank you." The front desk flashed the biggest smile at her as she walks away heading to the main door.

As she exits through the Claridge main entrance, gets back into her Aston Martin and speeds away.

Cradle is finally parking the Lincoln after almost being stuck in traffic for hour. No need for him to stop at the front desk. He proceeds straight up to his room via elevator and walks down the hall and slides his key and enters his room. Nothing appears to be out of place since the murderer has entered his room and left. He sat down in a brown leather wing chair, poured himself a cup of coffee. Hot, black and strong is how Cradle likes his coffee. The coffee's fresh full aroma, and hotness is definitely appeals to his palate.

He took a large sip of the black coffee, rocked forward and back. The chair was stationary, he created the rocking motion with his own body. He continued moving around the room until a painful whine from deep inside came from his lips and nose and caused him to violently throw his head forward, then back against the chair, He looked across the bed at a nearby table.

Standing unsteadily, the room seem to be spinning around like a top on a string and his vision got getting blurry that objects in the hotel room became morphed

o

together. He falls back on the bed like a fallen tree crashes down in the forest and he passes out cold. Thunder and lighting would not be enough to wake him from his deep drugged sleep.

Several hours later Cradle awakes from being drugged by the killer. He sat on edge of the bed, his elbows on his knees, and rubbed his eyes to refocused them His vision is 100% clear and back to normal as he looks around the hotel room. He thinks to himself that there was something in the black coffee I drank, but how can someone get into my room in which I am the only one with a key.

Cradle looks at the clock on the mantle it is now 3:00 p,m, Wow! I have lost 5 hour since I saw the killer go into Harrods, plant a tracking device on her car, follow her for a bit and then get caught in a traffic jam. Richard Royster's murderer is long gone now and I need to check out this hotel room and get back into my hot pursuit mode. He takes a shower, dress and packs his duffle bag to check out.

Fifteen minutes later, Cradle rode the elevator from the seventh floor to the Claridge's lobby He reluctantly hands the card key to the first desk clerk but not without asking him a pertinent question, " Did you let anyone have access to my room after I left this morning." "Yes , a woman came in, said she was your wife and wanted to surprise you in your room." Front desk clerk said. "What does this woman look?" "BTW I am not married." Cradle replied. "She was average height appeared to be Hispanic and Middle Eastern descent in facial features with long red flowing hair." Front desk clerk said. "That woman who let up in my room slipped a mickey in my coffee, I drank it and I was passed out for several hour." Cradle stated. " I am very sorry about that Detective Cradle.' Front desk clerk responded. " May I speak to your manager?" Cradle said. "Sure Detective Cradle." Front desk clerk responded.

The hotel manager came out of his office to the front desk in a matter of minutes. "Detective Cradle I apologize for my desk clerk allowing an intruder in your hotel room that resulting you being drugged, since it was our responsibility to secure your room at all times Claridge will cover the cost of your stay. No charge on your credit card."

o

"Thank you for your concern and generosity Sir." Cradle said. The hotel manager hands a Claridge hotel bill with 0.00 charges to Cradle just like he had said. Cradle extend his hand and shakes the hand of the hotel manager. He flashes a large toothy smile as he walks out of the main entrance. Things are looking up for him in London. Now it was time to get on with tracking the killer.

Cradle gets into the Lincoln, the tracking system is flashing constantly and emitting a loud bell striking sound similar to that of the famous Big Ben. He t aps the red button to shut it off and the small screen shows the whereabouts of the killer in Paris, France near the Eiffel Tower. Cradle has quickly grown weary of the tracking process since he lost so much time with the drugging and being passed out. He resets his GPS for new coordinates from 30 Davies Street to that of Paris, France. According to the GPS, Paris is 5 hours ,10 minutes and 290 miles away from London.

Cradle had no clue or idea that he was going to get a European tour of tracking Richard Royster's killer down as he drives down the street turning right on Brook Street, next right onto Bond Street, another right onto Bruton Street and at the end of the road making a left onto Berkeley Square. Keeping left on Berkeley Street, at the end of the road turning left onto Piccadilly, turning right into Saint James's Street. At end of the road, turning left onto Pall Mall, taking a sharp right turn onto Pall Mall, taking a slight left turn onto Marlborough Road and then turning left onto The Mall. Next, at the roundabout, taking the third exit onto Northumberland Avenue, turning left onto Victoria Embankment, continuing onto East Smithfield, The Highway and onto Leamouth Road for 3.2 miles. Now, taking a slight left turn onto Leamouth Road, turning left onto East India Dock Road, turning left onto A102 towards Lewisham, Blackwell Tunnel and continuing onto Rochester Way Relief Road for 3.2 miles. Cradle keeps right on M2 towards Dover, Channel Tunnel for the next 19.5 miles. Then, he takes exit 3 towards A229, Maidstone for 5.4 miles, at the roundabout, he takes the third exit towards the Channel Tunnel, V Crematorium for 0.5 miles.

o

Then 0.2 miles at the roundabout, he takes the first exit onto A229 towards Channel Tunnel, M20 and 2.2 miles turning left towards London, Ashford and 0.3 miles at the roundabout, taking the first exit to merge onto M20 towards Ashford, Channel Tunnel. For the next 30 miles he takes exit 11A towards Channel Tunnel, 1.7 miles he takes a slight left turn, 0.6 miles continue onto Folkestone-Calais.

He drives 33.9 miles along this country road, then keeping right for 1.1 miles merging onto A16 towards E15, A26 and for 4.1 miles taking the exit to merge onto A26 towards Saint-Omer, Arras. Then he drives for 96.2 miles before taking exit to merge onto E15 towards A3, Bordeaux, 1.2 miles keeping left to merge onto A3 towards A86 and keeping left for 1 mile to merge onto A3 towards A86, A4 and next 9 miles to exit left onto Boulevard Peripherique.

Next, Cradle drives another 3.3 miles before taking the exit to merge onto Quai de Bercy towards Paris-Centre, Porte de Bercy, 0.1 miles keeping onto Quai de Bercy towards Paris-Centre, Charenton-Bercy 2, 1.3 miles continuing onto Quai de la Rapee and 0.3 miles turning left onto Quai de la Rapee and 1.2 miles before turning onto Place de l'Hotel de Ville .

He goes for 302 feet before turning left onto Avenue Victoria in Paris, France at 9:20 pm He recalls from memory the last whereabouts of the killer was near the Eiffel Tower, so he reprograms his GPS system for Avenue Victoria to the Eiffel Tower which shows up on the screen to be 3.5 miles away and 15 minutes drive.

At this juncture in his trip, he is feeling very tired and weary from his long drive from London, he takes a sip of Coke Cola in which t he catches a second wind and decides to drive over to the Eiffel Tower anyway fighting back sleep.

Cradle make a right onto Boulevard de Sebastopol, then turning left onto Rue de Rivoli and keeps right for the next 2.7 miles. He makes a slight left turn at 0.2 miles into Place de Varsovie, turning left onto Pont d'Iena and turning right at 0.1 miles onto Quai Branly and 0.2 miles turning left onto Avenue de Suffren. He makes a left turn at 0.1 miles onto Avenue Octave Greard and prepare to park the Lincoln at 0.1 miles near Avenue Pierre Loti.

o

He open the door, steps out of the Lincoln, walking left on Avenue Pierre Loti and walking 72 feet then taking a left on Avenue Pierre Loti. Cradle does not see a silver Aston Martin parked anyway near the famous Paris landmark, The Eiffel Tower.

Cradle gazes up at the beautiful, majestic Eiffel Tower which was named after a contractor, engineer, architect and showman by the name of Gustave Eiffel completed on March 31, 1889. It is getting late by the passing hours and Cradle is already dead tired, he returns to the Lincoln and inputs data for query information on the nearest hotel. Four Seasons Hotel George V on 31 Avenue George V 1.2 miles 8 mins away from the Eiffel Tower.

He went down to end of road 0.2 miles, turning left onto Avenue de La Bourdonnais, then turning right onto Quai Branly for 0.1 miles. He goes 0.3 miles before turning left onto Pont de l'Alma and driving another 0.5 miles before taking a left turn onto Avenue George V.

Cradle spotted the Four Seasons ahead, parks his Lincoln in the driveway out front of the hotel. He get out of his car began walking towards the main entrance of the Four Seasons, stops at the front desk to reserve a room for the night. "May I help you Sir." the front desk said with a French accent. " I would like to reserve a room for the night." Cradle replied.

" I have a standard room available on the 8th Floor." front desk said. "Yes, that will work just fine." Cradle replied. "The room cost $250.00 francs." front desk responded. "Cradle hands the front desk clerk his Visa. "The front desk processes the credit card and hands him the key for room 800. "Thank you."

Cradle said and walks away towards the elevator. He took the elevator to the 8th floor of the Four Seasons. He walked less than 100 feet, put the key in the door to room 800 and enters the room. Cradle flips on the light switch in which turns on

o

the lamp on the night stand. He places his duffle bag in the chair, immediately he is stripping off his clothes, takes a nice hot shower and goes to bed. As soon as his head hits the pillow, he is out like a light.

Cradles awakes at 8:00 a.m., rolled out of bed, goes into the bathroom, takes a shower and shaves. He gets dressed, places a breakfast order for room service consisting of scrambled eggs with cheese, croissant, orange juice and coffee. He finishes breakfast by 9:00, and sat at the small table brought in by room service drinking seconds of coffee and reading a USA today paper for Friday, July 29, 1993. Enjoying an interlude he sensed must be very brief.

Now it was time for him to leave and get back on the case tracking down the killer. Cradle left the room and waited for the elevator to take him to the hotel lobby to check out the fabulous Four Seasons. Minutes later he is back in the Lincoln with flashing red alert on his tracking, he pushed the button and the screen shows the killer is now in Budapest, Hungary.

Cradle reprograms his GPS from the Four Seasons, Paris to Budapest, Hungary. The GPS shows 13 hours 39 minutes and 928 miles to drive there. He departs Paris at 10:00 am and arrives in Budapest at 11:40 pm. No question about it. Cradle is here in Budapest to captured Richard Royster's murderer and close the case finally.

The tracking system screens shows the killer is over at Buda castle. Buda castle is the historical castle and palace complex of the Hungarian kings in Budapest, and was first completed in 1265. In the past, it has been called Royal Palace and Royal Castle.

Cradle drives his Lincoln over to the Buda Castle, he pauses at the main entrance and looked around spotting the silver Aston Martin parked there for the moment. Now, the killer turns the ignition and starts up the Aston Martin's engine and speeds off like a bat out of hell. He trails right behind her, going 0.3 miles to the end of the road, turning right onto Tabor utca, turning left onto Miko utca, turning left onto Attila ut and then turning left onto Alagut utca. Then at the roundabout,

o

taking the second exit onto Clark Adam ter, keeping right on Szechenyi Istvan ter and keeping left to cross the Chain Bridge. The Szechenyi Chain Bridge is a suspension bridge that spans the River Danube between Buda and Pest and the first permanent bridge in Budapest. Now a monument is a fascinating spectacle that has attracted many tourists to Budapest. Killer is driving with excessive speeds upwards to 120 miles per hour as Cradle continues to trail her across the bridge. The Aston Martin being driven by the killer creens off the highway smashing into side of the bridge midway between Buda and Pest. The car flips upside down in the air and hits the water hard and submerges in Danube River. Cradle stops and parks his Lincoln on the bridge, get out and walks over to the side of the bridge to see the killer's car floating in the water.

The complexities in Royster's professional life, including that of being a secret agent, plus the total ultimate surprise with direct acquaintances were caught off guard by his sudden untimely demise. Therefore, leaving no credible conclusion but that he was murdered to keep his silence.

The barbaric blood sport does not always die with the victim. In death, Richard Royster became something he likely couldn't have possibly imagined in life: A hero and martyr to the Far Right.

Royster must be rolling over in his grave as his status as the ironic martyr of Reid administration, hero to the most extreme fringes of the far right.

Perhaps that's the most compelling counterargument against all the conspiracists, the complete lack of iron clad proof that stands up to the scrutiny linking Royster or the Reid's to any concrete nefarious plot.

Cradle is totally speechless from the events that just transpired. He had high hopes of bringing Richard Royster's killer to justice but no such luck. The killer is dead and the case file is closed.

o